The
WORST-CASE SCENARIO
Survival Handbook:
Junior Edition

The
WORST-CASE SCENARIO
Survival Handbook:
Junior Edition

By David Borgenicht and Robin Epstein
Illustrated by Chuck Gonzales

chronicle books · san francisco

A WORD OF WARNING: It's always important to keep safety in mind. If you're careless, even the tamest activities can result in injury. As such, all readers are urged to act with caution, ask for adult advice, obey all laws, and respect the rights of others when handling any Worst-Case Scenario.

Copyright © 2007 by Quirk Productions, Inc.

 A QUIRK PACKAGING BOOK.
All rights reserved.

Worst-Case Scenario and The Worst-Case Scenario Survival Handbook are trademarks of Quirk Productions, Inc.

iPod, Cheerios, and Jell-O are registered trademarks of Apple Computer, Inc., General Mills, Inc., and Kraft Food Holdings, Inc., respectively.

Book design by Lynne Yeamans.
Typeset in Adobe Garamond, Blockhead, and Imperfect.
Illustrations by Chuck Gonzales.

Library of Congress Cataloging-in-Publication Data
Borgenicht, David.
The worst-case scenario survival handbook : junior edition / by David Borgenicht and Robin Epstein ; illustrations by Chuck Gonzales.
p. cm. — (A Quirk packaging book)
ISBN 978-0-8118-6065-9
1. Social skills in children—Juvenile literature. 2. Socialization—Juvenile literature.
3. Children—Humor—Juvenile literature. I. Epstein, Robin, 1972– II. Gonzales, Chuck.
III. Title. IV. Series.
HQ783.B663 2007
646.700835—dc22
2007012511

Manufactured by Toppan Leefung, Da Ling Shan Town, Dongguan, China, in June 2010.

10 9 8 7 6 5 4

This product conforms to CPSIA 2008.

Chronicle Books LLC
680 Second Street, San Francisco, California 94107

www.chroniclekids.com

CONTENTS

CHAPTER 3

Survival Skills for Your Social Life

Introduction

You'll often hear adults say they wish they could be kids again. They say things like, "Oooh, childhood—such a delicious and carefree time of life! No responsibilities, nothing to worry about…why, it's practically perfection on a plate!"

Puh-lease!

After you've stopped snorting with laughter, don't you want to reply, "Um, *hello*? Earth to Oldie McMoldy! Do you *really* not recall what it's like to climb a mountain of homework every night? Could you have *possibly* forgotten what it's like to deal with the most annoying, wedgie-giving brother *ever*? Do you *honestly* not remember how hard it is to convince others *it wasn't you—it was the dog* that just farted right next to you?"

Being a kid is no cakewalk down Easy Street with an ice-cream cone in your hand. But there's plenty of fun to be had every day—as long as you know how to steer clear of the dog poo in your path. That's where this book comes in: It offers step-by-step instructions, clever comebacks, and excellent excuses that will help you breeze through tough times, side-stepping the poo with a smile on your face.

If you find yourself in a sticky situation at home—say, your allowance is skimpier than a teeny-weeny bikini, or your little sib won't stay out of your stuff—we have excellent solutions to help you deal. Maybe you got a bad report card, or it's picture day at school and you didn't know it—we've got strategies to help you cope. We even tackle the great outdoors, offering foolproof fixes if you have to walk to school in the worst weather or deal with things that sting.

If you experiment with some of the techniques we recommend, we bet you'll not only find some great solutions to life's little mysteries, you'll also have a blast!

—David Borgenicht and Robin Epstein

CHAPTER 1

Survival Skills at Home

How to Make Your Room Shipshape

If dirty laundry, trash, and toys are scattered all over your floor, these steps will help get the "CleanYour-RoomImmediately" monkeys off your back.

① Divide and conquer.

Start by finding all items of clothing and putting them into one pile. Next, gather up all pieces of trash and put them in a second pile. In a third pile, collect all your toys and the remaining random stuff.

② Scoop and dunk.

Scoop all the contents of pile number one into the nearest laundry hamper. Wheel a garbage can up to pile number two, and perfect your slam dunk as you toss all of your trash into it (making sure to recycle recyclables!). Finally, see pile number three just sitting there in the middle of your room? Give yourself ten minutes to put away as many things as you can.

3 **If you have anything left . . .**

Still looking at a pile of stuff? Well, you won't see it if you shove it under your bed, will you? So don't dilly-dally—put that pile where the sun don't shine.

4 **Make the bed by using the "breadspread."**

Making a bed that you're just going to mess up later that night feels like a time waster. So don't think of this as making your bed. Think of it as topping your bed sandwich with "breadspread." Find the exact middle of your bedspread or comforter and place it in the center

Place the middle of your bedspread
in the center of your bed.

Smooth down the spread.

Bin There, Done That!

Don't like chucking your stuff? Stacking crates, like the kind you buy at a housewares store—or the milk crates used at supermarkets—can be your best friend if you're the pack-rat type. You can store anything and everything in these bins. And because they stack on top of one another, they look tidy, which means you'll be able to fool people into thinking *you're* tidy, too.

of your bed. Now smooth down the spread so that its corners line up with the corners of the bed and the extra material drapes off the sides of the bed. *Voilà!* The results look good enough to eat!

5 Make like a dog and sniff out any remaining problems.

Starting at your door, get down on all fours, Fido-style. Let your nose lead you around the room to sniff out any overlooked socks or bags of cheese puffs. Dispose of your discoveries as appropriate.

6 Next time, convince, beg, or bribe someone to help you with the cleanup.

The more hands pitching in, the faster the job gets done. Old people realize this: That's probably why they had your younger sibling(s) in the first place. So recruit away. You might need to offer little sibs some sort of reward in exchange for their help. If so, tell them that by cleaning with you they'll learn the famous "make like a dog" trick (see step 5). The youngest of younger sibs might just go for that one!

> **BE AWARE** • Cleaning your room is a task that will need to be done again and again, unless you can think of a more permanent solution. You could take a vow of poverty and donate your possessions to charity, but that would mean giving away your favorite stuff. Or, you could try to convince your family that your mess is actually an art installation. It's okay if they don't completely grasp it—you are an avant-garde artist, which means you are ahead of the times.

How to Survive a Nosy Sibling

It's a fact of life: Brothers and sisters are always getting into each other's business. So, here's how to keep yours out of yours.

 Lights out.

Before leaving your room, unscrew all the light bulbs and pull your shades down. Store the bulbs in a dresser drawer for safekeeping and stash a flashlight there, too. When your sibling comes in, it'll be too dark for her to see anything.

 Let her know two can play the snooping game.

If Sis sneaks into your room, sneak into hers and "borrow" her favorite toy. When she demands you give it back, make her sign the "Staying Out of My Stuff" contract on page 126.

HOW TO KEEP YOUR JOURNAL SECRET

 Use a decoy journal.

Create a fake journal to throw the snooper off track, and hide it in a place you know the snooper will look. The entries in your fake journal should be believable enough that the snooper stops looking for the real journal. Or, you could address the snooper directly, like this: "I get the feeling my little bro found my journal. He's probably reading it now, *aren't you, snoop*?! "

 Hide your journal in a super-hard-to-find spot.

Snoopers search predictable spots: under your mattress, at the bottom of your desk drawer, or in your book bag. So, hide your journal behind books on your bookshelf, fold it into a sweater you keep at the bottom of your dresser drawer, or tape it under the lid of a random shoebox.

Places to Hide Your Journal

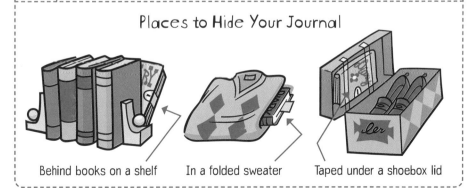

Behind books on a shelf　　In a folded sweater　　Taped under a shoebox lid

How to Survive Being Grounded

Grounding takes many forms, but it always starts the same way: An adult has gotten steamed, and now he's determined to make you feel the heat. Try these ideas to make that "heat" a little less punishing!

1 Pretend you agree with the decision to punish you.

Adults believe that grounding teaches you a lesson. "Agreeing" with the grounding makes them think the lesson is being learned. Say, "I understand why you're grounding me. And if I were in your shoes, I'd ground me, too." Hold your laughter until you are safely back in your room.

2 Sleep it off.

If you're sent to your room, remember there's a very comfortable bed in there. Take this time to chill out and daydream.

3 Do that project you keep meaning to do.

Think of this period of "punishment" as an opportunity to kickstart your art project/science experiment/future as a guitar god.

4 Do the jailhouse workout.

Prisoners know that doing push-ups makes the time go by more quickly, with the added bonus of making their upper bodies strong. Just imagine the look on your personal jailer's face when you emerge from your holding cell with bulging biceps!

⑤ Renegotiate the terms of your punishment.
Give the punisher some time to cool down, then calmly ask if she will consider letting you out early. Without cracking up, say, "I know what I did was wrong. I've learned my lesson. May I please be paroled?"

BE AWARE • After you've spent a couple of hours doing arts and crafts in your room, you might discover something alarming: You don't want to leave! Don't get too freaked out. This is a common reaction to imprisonment, and the cure is simple. As soon as you get released from the slammer, call a friend and plan to hang out.

Arguments to Make If Your Stuff Gets Taken Away

 Television privileges: "If I can't watch TV, I won't be able to watch the Learning Channel. You want me to learn, don't you?"

 Video game privileges: "I don't play video games for fun—I play them to improve my hand-eye coordination. Don't foil my attempts at coordination, please!"

 Skateboard privileges: "But I need my skateboard to get to the flower shop in order to buy you a 'You're the Best Parent Ever' bouquet."

 Outdoor privileges: "Wouldn't it be better if I worked off my excess energy outside instead of in here, near your fragile valuables?"

 Mall privileges: "But I finally saved enough of my babysitting money to buy you that waffle maker you've been eyeing."

 Cell phone privileges: "But what if I get lost, or need to call to let you know I'm going to be a little bit late?"

How to Clean Your Plate of Something You Hate

"Enjoy!" your friend's mom says as she serves you something smelling like dirty socks. "Bon appétit!" cries the waiter, handing you a plateful of something that looks and smells like cat food. "Eat up!" instructs Grandma, giving you meatloaf she baked her dentures into. When you're a prisoner at the dinner table, there's no escaping till you deal with that meal.

 ### Sauce it up.

Disguise the taste of something disgusting with a generous helping of something tastier. To avoid getting caught, put the condiment on the *side* of your plate instead of pouring it directly on your food. Use your fork to push bite-sized pieces through the pool of sauce. Now lift that forkful of yuck to your mouth and stay focused on the taste of the sauce—chew quickly, swallow, and repeat.

Top 10 Flavor Savers

Here's a list of condiments and sauces that can really disguise a foul food.

1. Ketchup
2. Mustard
3. Salsa
4. Spaghetti sauce
5. Gravy
6. Barbecue sauce
7. Applesauce
8. Soy sauce
9. Tartar sauce
10. Relish

Sauce your food less obviously, of course!

 Breathe to relieve.

Once you start chewing, begin blowing air out of your nose in quick, short bursts. Concentrating on your breathing not only gets you to think less about the food, it prevents you from smelling it. The end result? You'll barely be able to taste it (because taste and smell are linked).

Flush it away.

If your meal is so bad that swallowing it is making you gag, then turn to your best ally in this situation: your drink. Chew a small portion of food at a time, and then take a sip of your drink to ease it down.

Bread it.

A simple dinner roll can be a lifesaver when you're faced with a dreadful dinner. Bread is especially good when you don't like the texture of your food (like if it's slimy). Just take a bite of bread with every bite of slime. The blandness of the bread will also help mask bad flavors.

Practice "Mind Over Meal."

In extreme cases, you may need to call upon your imagination. Consider it a challenge to see if you can imagine that the liver you're eating is actually a delicious grilled steak.

> **BE AWARE** • When food is spicy, drink milk instead of water to lessen the burn. Another heat-beater is buttered bread—the fat in the butter counteracts the heat.

Disguise it with mashed potatoes.

If you really can't deal with the taste, the thick white-ness of mashed potatoes provides the perfect cover for the horror on your plate. Lift the mashed potatoes with your fork, and slide that unwanted crud under the cloud of mashed mush using your knife. Other useful places to stow food are under a helping of peas or chunky applesauce. Try cutting your food into tiny pieces first—this makes it easier to hide.

How to Increase a Skimpy Allowance

You need more dough, simple as that. Here's how to get your parents to agree that you deserve a raise.

⭐ Compare the going rate.

Find out how much allowance your friends get. Then write up a chart to show that you've done your research and your wages are lagging.

Money-Saving Tips to Make Do with What Ya Got

- **Create a budget and stick to it.**
  Decide you won't spend any more than *X* dollars a day.

- **Carry around very little cash.**
  If you don't have it on hand, you can't throw it away.

- **Keep a change jar and make daily deposits.**
  All those nickels and dimes add up.

- **Don't buy anything.**
  Sometimes the most obvious tip is the best of all.

 Acknowledge that with greater money comes greater responsibility.
Offer to spend more time with your annoying little sister if you get a pay bump.

 Be your own union.
Just like a labor union, negotiate for fixed raises once a year. Your birthday would be the perfect occasion.

Top 5 Ways to Get More Dough

1. Go couch diving.
Couch cushions are a magnet for change. Pull them up, and you're likely to locate some coins hiding deep in the couch cracks.

2. Do odd jobs.
Is it winter? Shovel snow for dough. Is it spring? Water the flowers for that green. Is it summer? Fan your family for some coin. Is it fall? Rake leaves for legal tender.

3. Rent out your toys.
If you're not playing with a certain toy anymore, rent it to another kid for a week and charge a set fee.

4. Teach old folks how to use electronic equipment.

People used to say, "You can't trust anyone over thirty." Now people say, "You can't trust anyone over thirty to set up their own computer equipment." Offer your services to the nearest technically challenged oldster and teach her how to master her cell phone or laptop.

5. Become a short-order cook.

Offer to make special brown-bag creations for your classmates. They'll be glad to avoid the grub the cafeteria is serving.

How to Make Your Younger Sibling Bearable

Isn't it amazing how such little kids can be such big pains in the butt? Of course, *you* were young once, but you've grown out of it—so maybe there's hope for your smaller sibling, too. When you and Little You have to hang out together, there's no reason it can't be fun for the both of you ... especially if you figure out how to mold your sib into the perfect personal assistant.

Turn your sibling into a pack mule.

Tell your younger sib that if he's going to hang with you, he has to carry your backpack. And spare pieces of clothing in case you get cold. And your sweater if you get hot. If you want to be nice, tell him he doesn't *have* to carry your stuff on his head…but he'll get bonus points that way.

 Make your sibling your personal messenger service.

In a time of e-mails and texts, it's unusual to get a hand-written note. Have a little sib hand-deliver your notes for you. It adds that extra-special personal touch that says, "I care enough to send my sister."

 Insist that your sibling become your server.

Hungry? Thirsty? Just want a little snack? Sure, you could walk to the refrigerator to get that food or drink. Then again, why not have little bro do it for you? Tell him you're teaching him a skill he can use later in life when his career as a movie star doesn't work out.

BE AWARE • Make sure your sib knows that working for you is an honor. To prevent her from getting the idea that this will be a regular thing, have her sign a contract stating that she gets that this is a one-time-only deal (see the "Hang Time" contract on page 127). Also, make sure she understands that children in other countries would fight for the opportunity to spend time with you.

Top 10 Reasons You Shouldn't Be Saddled with Your Sib

1. Her nose runs even when she's sitting still.

2. He chews with his mouth open.

3. She's covered in crumbs!

4. He smells like milk.

5. She somehow manages to make things sticky just by looking at them.

6. He turns everything into a song, then sings it really loudly.

7. She keeps calling you by a nickname you don't want anyone to know.

8. He never qualifies for the "You need to be this tall to get in" rides.

9. Her Cheerios spill EVERYWHERE!

10. He can't even work a video game controller.

How to Soothe a Peeved Parental Unit

When an adult in your life is mad, your life gets harder (even if you weren't the one who got him or her ticked off). These ideas may make the dark clouds hanging over your parent's head pass faster.

1 Say the two all-purpose, virtually never-fail magic words: "I'm sorry."

Even if you're 100 percent sure you did nothing wrong, just say it. Then cock your head to the side, make your best puppy-dog eyes, and say it again as sincerely as possible: "I'm really, *really* sorry."

2 Avoid saying, "Wow, being angry at me really makes you look ridiculous."

Even though this might cross your mind, this sort of commentary is sure to refuel the flames of Mom's or Dad's anger. Refer to step 1 again for the only words you should be uttering right now.

Telltale Signs You've Got an Annoyed Adult on Your Hands

- Steam is pouring out of his nose or ears.

- Her arms are crossed and her foot is tapping, but there's no music playing in the background.

- She keeps pounding the kitchen table with her shoe.

- He's opening doors just so he can slam them shut.

- She's muttering to herself about living on a desert island with no distractions. No clutter. And no one else there to bother her!

- He's fluffing the pillows on the couch so loudly you can hear him three rooms away.

3 Give that madman or crazy lady some room.

Now that you've offered an apology, let Foul-Mood Morris or Mary have some space to be alone with his or her anger. Back away quietly and try not to do anything irritating.

4 Offer comfort ... comfort *food*, that is.

Prepare the person's favorite snack and leave it in a place where you know he'll find it. Include a simple note containing a heart and your initials.

5 Do something nice for Mr. or Ms. Angry Pants.

Complete the chore you're always being bugged to do without being asked to do it. Your parents will not only be pleasantly surprised, they'll know it's a sign that you want to make things better.

> **BE AWARE** • Sometimes being nice can backfire and lead to more punishment for no good reason. Continually gauge the mood of the parent in question, and back off if things seem to be heading south.

CHAPTER 2

Survival Skills at School

How to Ride the Bus without Getting Schooled

As if the fact that it delivers you to school weren't bad enough, the school bus can be a torture chamber on wheels. Spitballs fly, homework gets stolen, and wet willies are delivered at an alarming rate. But if you properly prepare yourself for the ride, you can turn your school bus into a mobile pleasure pad.

1 When boarding the bus, keep your head low but your eyes up.

This "modified turtle" positioning system alerts others that you're too cool to care what they're up to. You'll just walk to your seat, tough exterior shell in place, and no one will bother you.

2 Scope out the seat real estate.

Location is everything. First look for your friends, and if they're there, go sit with them. If you don't know anyone, an empty seat near the middle of the bus is your best bet. Steer clear of the far back, home to those who think they're hot stuff, and the far front, home to those who might consider the bus driver one of their best friends.

③ Turn on. Tune out.

Stick your ear buds in your ears, turn your music player on, and tune out the rest of the madness. Enjoy the relaxing sounds of your favorite tunes till the wheels of the bus stop rolling.

> **BE AWARE •** Some bus drivers assign seats on the first day of school, so it's important to choose your seat carefully that day.

Turtle

"Modified Turtle"
Positioning System

How to Get By When You're Late to Class

You don't know exactly how it happened, but you're late again! This is not good. If your teacher catches you, you're going to be in *big* trouble. That's why you're not going to get caught.

OPTION FOR THE BOLD: SNEAK IN

1 Lay the groundwork.

This option requires advance preparation. If there are any classes that you're likely to run late for, choose a friend who will be your accomplice. Then discuss the plan (see below) with your friend, and prepare a signal system you'll use when the need arises.

2 Get the attention of your friend inside.

If the classroom door is still open when you arrive, try to catch your friend's eye without calling attention to yourself. Make sure to avoid looking at the teacher or standing in the teacher's line of sight.

3 Give your friend the "Tell me when" signal. This will let him know that it's time to watch for the right moment for your entrance. Good moments include when the teacher is writing on the board, when the teacher is talking privately with another student, or anytime the teacher is just not focused on the door. When the moment is right, your friend should give you the "Go" signal.

4 As soon as you get the "Go" signal, go for it! Crouch low to the ground and make your way to your desk as quickly and quietly as you can. If your desk is far away from the door, see if there's a closer empty desk where you can make a pit stop. (And if you get caught, see more options on the next page!)

OPTION FOR THE SLIGHTLY LESS DARING: GIVE AN EXCUSE

⭐ **I'm a comedian in training!**
Say, "I'm not late ... I was trying to make an entrance!"

⭐ **I'm just trying to be a model citizen.**
Tell the teacher, "I would have been here sooner, but I know we're not supposed to run in the halls."

⭐ **I'm a VIP!**
Offer your apologies—you had an early-morning audition that took *forever*.

⭐ **I forgot to reset my watch.**
Tell the teacher, "I'd be right on time if this school were in Kansas City!"

⭐ **I'm hurt!**
Enter crying, limping, and explaining that you just fell down the stairs.

BE AWARE • Before you attempt to use the last excuse, make sure your school has stairs.

How to Survive Going "Splat" in the Cafeteria

The only thing worse than being forced to eat a school lunch is tripping while carrying it on your tray in the cafeteria. The good news: Now that your food's gone flying, you don't have to swallow it. The bad news: Everyone in school just saw you "eat it." Here's how to make that trip a little less bitter.

1 Pop up and dust off.

Stand up as soon as you can. The faster you can get up, the faster this nightmare is over. If you've spilled any food on yourself, or if you have skid marks down your pant legs, wipe yourself off to minimize the evidence that you were just airborne.

2 Scan the room for the reaction.

Determine if your fall was something only a few people noticed, or if it was seen and heard by every person in the cafeteria, including, but not limited to: other students, teachers, administrators, visitors, lunch ladies, and the janitor.

3 Laugh it off and take your bow.

Laugh at yourself. That way, if others join in, they're now laughing *with* you instead of *at* you. Then, if the whole cafeteria's watching, prove that you have a great sense of humor by taking a big bow. If only a small group of people saw the event, simply give them a salute and nod your head.

4 With your chin up, walk to your table and eat what remains on your tray.

To minimize embarrassment, do not dwell in your puddle of spilled milk. Walk away and sit down with your friends as soon as you can.

Top 5 Things to Yell After You've Hit the Ground

1. "Man down!"
2. "Food fight!"
3. "Duck and cover!"
4. "Thar she blows!"
5. "Stop, drop, and roll!"

How to Ace a Spelling Test without Spell-Check

Spelling isn't directly related to intelligence, but it is directly related to how we remember things. So here are some tricks that will help you recall words that you still feel like a nincompoop for mispelling—er, misspelling.

1 Come up with a clever memory aid.

These are known as mnemonic (pronounced "nih-MON-ick") devices. Say you have to write a thank-you note. Do you write it on stationery or stationary? Remember *E* is for "envelope," so it's *stationery*. Is it a school principle or principal? It's *principal* because he's your "pal." *Separate* or *seperate*? Remove "a rat" by "sep-a-rat-ing" it.

2 Sound it out, out loud.

By breaking the word into pieces, it becomes less scary.

3 Write the word in the air.

In a spelling-bee setting, you don't have the advantage of seeing how the word looks on the written page. Try writing the word in big letters in the air in front of you. This will help you visualize what you're trying to spell.

BE AWARE • Here is a list of commonly misspelled words. Don't let them fool you!

- apparent
- believe
- conscience
- discipline
- embarrass
- fiery
- guarantee
- hierarchy
- inoculate
- jewelry
- kernel
- license
- millennium

- necessary
- occurrence
- privilege
- questionnaire
- rhythm
- sergeant
- twelfth
- until
- vacuum
- weird
- xylophone
- yucca
- zoology

Source: www.yourdictionary.com

How to Survive a Trip to the Principal's Office

You may be guilty, you may be innocent, but there will be no trial: For you the principal is judge and jury. So when you get sent to his office, be lawyer-like and present your best case.

Neat hair

Clean shirt

Shined shoes

PRINC

1 Dress like you're going to court.

Since you probably can't change into a suit, make what you're wearing look more respectable: Tuck in your shirt, tie your shoes, smooth down your hair, and do your best to get that "you can't catch me" grin off your face.

2 Silently listen to the charges against you.

Don't butt in while the principal is talking. If you speak up while he's telling you what you've been accused of, you risk two things. One: giving away too much information. Two: ticking him off. So keep your trap shut.

Random Excuses to Offer the Principal When Nothing Else Is Working

- "I'm just trying to make my classmates look good."

- "I was sleepwalking."

- "Picasso didn't do his best work until he was in his seventies."

- "I'm so upset about the [insert major world current event] situation. It's affecting me terribly."

3 Address the principal with respect.

When it's your turn to talk, remember your manners and say your "please"s and "thank you"s, your "yes, ma'am"s and "no, sir"s. Since you're trying to convince the principal you're innocent, the more respectful you act, the less criminal you'll seem.

Maintain eye contact.

Don't blink.

Listen silently.

4 Maintain eye contact.

Guilty parties tend to look down and away. By looking the principal directly in the eye, you'll appear more trustworthy. And don't blink too much—excessive blinking is a sign of lying.

5 Don't be a rat.

Don't blame someone else or use a classmate as a scapegoat. You want to get cleared of these charges, but not at the expense of another kid.

6 When asked what happened, explain it quickly and clearly.

Don't blah-blah-blah—the principal has heard a *million* excuses. Give him your side of the story, outlining details that present you in the best light.

7 Wrap it up with "sincere" thanks.

End your speech by thanking the principal for listening to your side and judging the situation fairly. (Adults love being appreciated for doing their job. Plus, saying "thank you" will make him feel guilty about inflicting harsh punishment.)

How to Survive a Bad Report Card

Grades happen. If your report card is covered in letters that cling to the lower end of the grading alphabet, here's how to reduce its impact when you hand it to an adult for their signature.

1 Be affectionate and complimentary but not obviously fake.

If your flattery before handing over the report card is too over-the-top, your signer will smell something's up. Find a medium-sized compliment (something big enough to put her in a good mood, but not so big that it's obviously a lie) and give it with a smile.

2 Ask your signer to sit down—there's something you need to discuss.

Make sure she takes a comfy chair—you sit in something wooden and uncomfortable—then say you have something you need to talk to her about.

Top 3 Medium-Sized Compliments

1. "I don't think I've ever told you this before, but I think you've got a great sense of style."

2. "You are so much cooler than [insert name of friend or neighbor]'s [mom/dad]."

3. "You look like you've lost weight."

3 Begin listing a series of real-life unfortunate events.

Remind your signer that awful things are going on in the world, such as war, famine, and puppy torture. Then say, "All things considered, what I'm about to show you is not so bad."

4 Present the report card, look down, and admit that no one is more disappointed in you than you.

Say this without laughing.

5 If your signer clasps her chest and falls off her chair after seeing your grades, call 911.

While you wait for the ambulance, assure her that the report card is not really all that important, and that what she needs to focus on now is recovering.

6 Place the pen in her hand and have her sign at the X.

Before she's carted away, move her hand to sign the report card. Promise your signer that you will do better next term, and try to mean it.

Successful Folks Who Bombed in School

- **Woody Allen,** an Academy Award–winning writer, producer, and director, flunked motion picture production and English at New York University.

- **Napoleon Bonaparte,** one of the greatest military figures of all time, finished near the bottom of his class at military school.

- **Albert Einstein,** one of the world's greatest scientists, did terribly in elementary school, and failed his first college entrance exam.

- **William Faulkner,** a Nobel Prize–winning author, didn't graduate from high school because he didn't have enough credits.

- **Robert Kennedy,** former attorney general of the United States, failed first grade.

How to Get a Decent Photo on Picture Day

Most embarrassments fade fast. But a bad school photo lasts forever. Don't get caught looking like a weirdo in the yearbook. You'll never—and we mean *never*—live it down.

1 Water can help a bad hair day.

Woke up with crazy bed head? Realized you got hat head on the way to school? If you have no gel, try a tiny amount of hand lotion. Or simply go to the bathroom and wash your hands in warm water. Instead of drying them with a paper towel, run them through your hair.

2 Camouflage that pimple.

Remember, the size of your photo in the yearbook will be small. So even a *massive* zit will only be a mini-dot in the picture. The key is in minimizing its redness. If you have cover-up, lightly dot it around the area and smooth it into your skin.

3 Avoid patterns, stripes, or logos in favor of simple shirts in solid colors.

Go for light or bright solids that will make you stand out against the backdrop. Too much activity around your neckline distracts from the real subject of the photo—you! And besides, this year's coolest band could be next year's disgrace.

4 Use your best "I have a secret" smile.

The look on your face is by far the most important part of a yearbook picture. If you look happy or amused, the picture will turn out great. Think about the last time you laughed really hard. Be in *that* moment as the photo is being snapped.

Smile Examples

| The "Saber-Toothed Tiger" Grin | The "Smiling Is Hard" Look | The "I Have a Secret" Smile |
| (NOT Recommended) | (NOT Recommended) | (Recommended) |

How to Eat Lunch by Yourself...and Enjoy It

No one to sit with at lunch? As long as you're properly prepared with things to distract yourself, it's really no big whoop. Plus, when you've got something cool going on, you may find people wanting to sit with you to see what it is!

Read something fun.

This is "you" time, so use it to read something interesting—a book, magazine, instruction manual, whatever.

Play a game or do a puzzle.

Sudoku, solitaire, and crossword puzzles are all one-person activities, so it's better that there's no one there to distract you anyway.

Do origami.

If you can't make a swan, at least try folding a fan.

Create the best music playlist ever.

Then come up with other "best ever" lists, like "best movies ever," "best pets ever," "best books ever," and so on.

Start writing your memoirs.

Call it what you want—diary writing, journaling, or memoir writing—it's always cool to have a record of your thoughts and daily activities. You never know: Years from now what you're writing might be what someone reads during *his* lunch period!

Draw your own map of the world.

Invent names for new countries, like Mybuttissosorenya and Boredoutofmyheadistan.

Pretend you're a private eye.

Like Harriet the Spy, take notes on what other people in the lunchroom are doing to improve your powers of observation for future espionage jobs.

How to Give an Oral Report without Passing Out

People list public speaking as the scariest thing in the world—even scarier than being eaten by an alligator. But it's not *that* bad. At most, it causes a few minutes of discomfort (whereas getting eaten by an alligator could, theoretically, go on for *hours*). These tips will make those minutes fly by.

1 Rehearse your material.

Being nervous only means you care about what you're about to say, so practice your report until you're comfortable with it. Rehearse it in front of a mirror. Rehearse it in front of your computer screen. Rehearse it in front of a friend. Rehearse when you're in the shower, before you go to bed, and when you wake up. After all that rehearsing, doing the real thing will seem as routine as brushing your teeth.

2 Warm up and chill.

Focus on your breathing. Inhale for three seconds, then exhale for three seconds. If you can excuse yourself to the bathroom right before your turn to speak, do some stretching exercises to help you relax.

3 No disclaimers.

No disclaimers means: never apologize, and don't announce, "This is going to be terrible!" These things just plant the idea that your presentation will be terrible (which it won't). Likewise, don't tell people you're nervous, because if you've followed steps 1 and 2 they won't know you're nervous unless you tell them.

4 Picture yourself giving a speech that's the cat's pajamas.

Imagine yourself in front of the class, speaking slowly, clearly, and smartly. If you can see it, you can be it!

5 Remember, your audience wants you to do well.

Since no one wants to sit through a bad, boring speech, it follows that most people genuinely want you to succeed. And if you suspect that there are a few meanies who *aren't* rooting for you, remember that doing well is your best revenge. So just to spite them, ace this talk!

Harness the Power of Creative Visualization

- **Picture the whole class dressed up like bunny rabbits.** What could be scary about bunnies?

- **Pretend you are an important historical figure.** You are giving a speech so powerful it wins the election or ends the war. Important historical figures don't slump or say "umm," so thinking of them should help you deliver your speech with dignity.

- **See yourself taking a deep bow when you are finished.** Imagine how deeply relieved you will feel.

6 Focus on the subject of your speech, not the fact that you're giving one.

Concentrate on the topic you're talking about. Think about all the interesting aspects of the subject that you want to get across to your listeners. This will help you think less about the fact that you're delivering a speech.

7 Focus on the horizon.

Instead of looking at someone who might make a face at you, keep your eyes focused just above your audience's heads.

> **BE AWARE** • Remind yourself to breathe—it makes you pause and slow down so that people can understand what you're trying to say. And if you remember to breathe, you'll avoid hyperventilating.

CHAPTER 3

Survival Skills for Your Social Life

How to Get Beyond a Bully

Bullies have been around since the time of the caveman. As soon as the first caveman realized (1) he was hungry and (2) he was bigger than the caveman next to him who was innocently eating a sandwich, the bully was born. Today's bullies still resemble that primitive man. It's time for you to teach them to evolve.

★ Don't try to out-bully the bully.

Being jerky back to the bully isn't smart (even if it seems so at the time). Bullies have bad reputations because they do bad things. Don't sink to their level.

★ Don't show fear or anger.

Bullies love nothing more than seeing their victims freak out. Your best reaction is to stay cool. You may be scared, but try to keep a straight face, a firm voice, and a nonshaky stance. This will show the bully you're just no fun to hassle.

Say "Stop," then walk away.

Simple but effective: Just tell the bully to knock it off. She knows that bullying is wrong, but since most kids won't tell her to stop, she'll keep doing it. When you say "Stop," it forces her to think about what she's doing.

Make a joke of it if you can.

It's hard to make fun of someone if she's doing a better job of making fun of herself. In fact, lots of professional comics got their starts trying to make bullies laugh. If people think you're funny, they'll be more interested in hearing your jokes than in hurting your feelings.

Make a Joke Out of It

When passing through bully territory, try to travel with a pal.

It's true: There is safety in numbers. Try not to be alone around the bully. Ever.

 Get help from someone even bigger— an adult.

If, after ignoring the bully, he just won't stop bothering you, let an adult know about it. A teacher, a parent, a guidance counselor—any of these people might be able to step in and make things better. Tell the person about the problem and then the two of you can figure out how to handle the situation without making it worse.

 Get support from your fans.

Let your true friends know what's going on, and talk about the bully situation with them. Then keep your friends in mind whenever the bully makes you feel down or stressed out. Remember that no matter what the bully says, you still have your cheering section. And *they're* the ones who really matter!

How to Make Friends When You're the New Kid on the Block

When you're new to town and know *no* one, life can seem like no fun. But think of this as a chance to start fresh. In a new town (or a new school), you can be whoever you want to be, including the most popular person around.

1 Walk with confidence.

You may be scared out of your mind on your first day at a new school, but try to be like an actor and act fearless. Keep your head up as you walk, make eye contact with other students, and then smile at them. If you can look cool and in control, people will believe you are. You might even convince yourself.

2 When meeting people, lead with a compliment.

People love getting compliments. Tell someone you meet that you like his shirt or hair. Then let the conversation unfold naturally.

3 Do the "Hello, my name is _____" routine. Introduce yourself to the students sitting around you in homeroom. Say hello to the person whose locker is next to yours. Give a nod of the head and a smile to anyone who looks in your direction. If she nods or smiles back, find out what her name is.

4 Think of each day as a level in a video game. In any online role-playing game, you meet new people every day. You know advancing takes time, but you do so by learning the needs and wants of those around you. A new school is just like the start of a new game. Stay focused and play to win!

Fake It Till You Make It

Be prepared: It takes time to meet new people, and it takes even more time to meet new people that you actually click with. So until you have a group of friends you're proud to call your own, here are some ideas to help you deal with any awkward alone times.

- **Look casual.** Read a comic book, chill to your iPod, or customize your cell phone. You'll enjoy yourself and up your chances of attracting people with similar interests.

- **Try the old "I'm late for a very important appointment" routine.** If there's no one to hang with and you're getting bored or self-conscious, look up like you just forgot something, check your watch, and walk away quickly.

How to Survive Farting in Public

Call it what you will—a butt burp, a cheek flapper, a trouser trumpet, breaking wind, or cutting the cheese—sometimes you've just got to let one rip. Here are a few ways to keep people from thinking that you've got a lion roaring in your underpants.

The farter continues normal activity and provides no expression of guilt.

Block that fart!

Depending on where you are, grab a towel, jacket, or sweatshirt (anything made of thick, bulky fabric will do). Place it behind your behind and fart into it. The fabric will help mute the sound and absorb the smell. Now get as far away from that smelly towel as quickly as you can.

Cough-a-fart!

If you feel as if you're about to let a fanny bubble fly, start coughing very loudly. Keep coughing until after you've finished making that "joyful noise."

Put on your best "Who, me?" look.

Say you've launched a fart of the SBD (silent but deadly) variety, and it's not immediately obvious who brought the stink. Don't yell, "P-U! That smells!" because everyone knows that he who smelt it dealt it. Just quietly make a "wasn't me" face to disassociate yourself from the smell.

BE AWARE • If you're coughing, even though *you* can't hear the fart, others still might. So just to be on the safe side, if you're sitting down, try moving the chair to make its legs scrape the floor at the same time.

What to Say After You've Launched an Air Biscuit

If, despite your best efforts, your fart goes public, try saying one of these lines to turn it into a joke.

- "Well, there's no point in having a tush if you can't let it rejoice in song!"

- "Keep calling, sir! We'll find you!"

- "Hey, did somebody step on a duck?"

Fart Facts

- The average person farts about 14 times a day—whether she realizes it or not.

- Boys and girls fart with the same degree of frequency.

- Because cows graze on gas-inducing grass, they release so much methane gas every day that their farts contribute to global warming.

How to Outsmart a Prankster

The bottom line is this: If you want to learn how to stop pranksters in their tracks, you must first learn their tricks.

GIVING A WEDGIE

1 Prankster casually approaches his victim.

He can either sneak up on the victim from behind or cause a distraction. Example: He drops a pen, then asks the victim to pick it up.

2 The prankster grabs the victim's underpants and yanks them straight to the heavens.

The prankster digs for the top edge of the victim's briefs and pulls them as high as he can, just like he's pulling up a sock.

3 Prankster runs for the hills.

FOILING THE WEDGER

⭐ Wear low riders.

Fold the waistband of your underpants down until they ride low on your hips.

⭐ When the prankster has you by the waistband, yell, "Look out behind you!"

Because the prankster already has wedgies on the brain, he might assume he's about to get wedged himself. In his surprise, he may turn around and release you.

GIVING A WET WILLIE

1 Prankster licks her index fingers.

The prankster might pretend she's about to whistle with her fingers, sticking her index fingers in her mouth and licking them till they're good and wet.

2 Prankster approaches her victim, leans in, and squints at his or her nose.

By staring at another part of the victim's face, she'll take the "vic" by surprise.

3 As victim goes cross-eyed, trying to see what the prankster is looking at, prankster sticks her wet fingers into victim's ears.

The wet-willie giver will then twist those fingers around several times.

4 Prankster runs for the hills.

FOILING YOUNG WILLIAM

 Know the usual suspects.

Pranksters are a special breed, especially the kind that have wet willies in their repertoire. (Who wants someone else's earwax on their fingers?) So keep a mental list of these potential prank perpetrators, and when one of them starts squinting at your nose, step away "willie" fast!

 Pants the prankster mid-willie.

If you *do* get "willied," try to retaliate. Since the prankster's hands will be busy in your ears, he'll be defenseless. Take this time to yank his pants down.

Things You Can Do to Stop Yourself from Screaming

Prank pulling is only fun when it gets a great reaction—like a blood-curdling scream. So if you can practice *not* shrieking like a banshee, chances are, your days as a prank victim are running out. Here's how to avoid giving the prankster the satisfaction.

• Bite down on your lip.

• Cover your mouth with both hands.

• Close your eyes tightly and think of a walrus.

• Turn the scream into the first notes of the national anthem.

How to Make a Quick Fix on a Fashion Disaster

Your pants split. Your zipper broke. You've got a *giant* gob of gum in your hair. Whatever your problem, it doesn't have to be a disaster.

SPLIT PANTS

You just bent down to tie your shoe, and you heard *RRRRIP!* Here's what to do to keep your undies out of view.

⭐ Mask it.

If you can locate masking tape (or duct tape), tape over the split. Then, use the next technique to cover the tape (since tape isn't much of a fashion statement!).

⭐ Wrap it.

Take your coat, sweater, or an extra shirt and wrap it around your waist, knotting the sleeves in front.

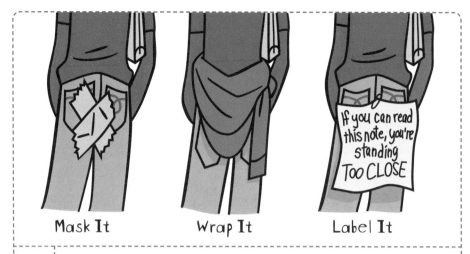

Mask It   Wrap It   Label It

 Label it.

If all else fails, tape a sign to your butt that says, "If you can read this note, you're standing too close."

GUM IN YOUR HAIR

You've just blown your biggest-ever bubble. But as it bursts, your greatest achievement turns into a gummy nightmare. Tons of gum is now stuck in your hair. But don't reach for the scissors yet—try these ideas first.

 Dab the gummed-up hair with cotton balls soaked in rubbing alcohol.

Rubbing alcohol reduces the stickiness of the gum and helps it slide off your hair.

Rub in some peanut butter.

Leave the peanut butter on the gummed-up hair for a few minutes. Now you should be able to rub the gum out. Wash your hair as soon as possible to remove the peanut butter smell!

Apply baby oil or olive oil.

The gum should slide right off.

BROKEN ZIPPER

Sometimes the problem with a zipper is that it keeps sliding down. Other times the stupid thing just won't go up. Both problems can be solved with a safety pin. (For this reason, it's always a good idea to keep a safety pin or two stowed in a pocket of your book bag. If you don't have one, though, ask a teacher if he or she has an extra one lying around.)

Don't call attention to the problem!

Instead, calmly slide a textbook (or binder or backpack) over your fly to cover the area. Then, as coolly as possible, excuse yourself to the bathroom, where you can deal with the problem in private.

For the sliding zipper, create a no-slip handle.
Hook the safety pin through the square opening at the bottom of the zipper pull. Now tug the zipper as high up as it will go and pierce it through the fabric on the top side of your fly. Pinch the pin closed.

 For the no-budge zipper, create a "butterfly" closure.
Pierce the safety pin through the middle of the outer edge of your fly. Now pierce the pin through the fabric on the outside edge of your zipper and close the pin. Yes, you'll have a safety pin through the middle of your fly, but this will allow you to keep your privates private till you can change pants.

"Butterfly" Closure

No-Slip Handle

How to Take the Bite out of Braces

Sure, you know there's a pearly white light at the end of the tunnel. The straight teeth you're going to have when your braces come off will look incredible! But right now you've got a mouthful of metal—or "clear" plastic—and it ain't pretty (especially not after a meal). Still, there's no need to be ashamed of that tin grin. If you follow these steps, you can flash your grill with pride.

 Brusha, brusha, brusha.
Braces tend to be food magnets, and you can often find a second meal from what gets trapped in your brackets alone. Pretty gross. Plus, trapped food makes your breath stink. The key is brushing your braces after every meal. But brushing isn't nearly as annoying as you might imagine, especially if you try to think of it as a chance to enjoy a minty-fresh dessert. (This will require some imagination on your part.)

Choose foods that soothe.

There's no way to sugarcoat the fact that your teeth will hurt when you first get braces. But that doesn't mean you have to limit yourself to things you can suck up with a straw. Treats like ice cream, pudding, and Jell-O are great for sore mouths. And guess what? They taste great, too!

Don't drool, fool!

Yep, it's true that you drool more when you have braces. This is because the braces trick your mouth into thinking you've got food in there. And since you're not going to put a sponge in your mouth to stop the saliva flow, keep a handkerchief handy to wipe off your chin every now and then.

> **BE AWARE •** Attempts to hide your braces (covering your face with your hair or never smiling) will only backfire. People will start to wonder why you're always moping. Braces are only temporary, so while you have them, wear them with pride.

Top 5 Foods to Avoid
Till You're Braces Free

Once upon a time, before you got your braces, these foods were fun to eat. Now they're just a sticky glue that's sure to get stuck in your wires.

1. Corn on the cob
2. Popcorn balls
3. Gum
4. Taffy
5. Caramel apples

If you know you'll be unable to resist gooey treats, carry an "interproximal brush" with you. This cone-shaped brush is designed to access tricky spots. Clean your braces right after eating, before food can harden.

How to Shake, Rattle, and Roll through a School Dance

Last place you wanted to be was at a school dance. But for whatever reason, here you are, in the school gymnasium, feeling unsure of what to do next. Since you definitely don't want your art teacher to ask you for a pity dance, you need to act fast.

IF YOU WANT TO DANCE...

 Ease into the groove.

If you're not all that comfortable on the dance floor, take it slow at first. You don't have to move a lot to be "dancing." Simple is good—maybe just a side-to-side sway with a little bounce to the beat. Use this time to scope out the dance floor. If you see a decent dancer, study that person's moves and see which ones you can ... ahem ... steal.

BE AWARE • While dancing, it's important to avoid the bad habit known as "the overbite," when you bite your lower lip with your front teeth. Keep your mouth relaxed and *smile* instead.

Smile, baby!

Your smile is by far your best dance move. It makes people *want* to dance with you, and it spreads the good times around (smiles are extremely contagious). And if you start to worry about what people think of your dance maneuvers, smile *more*. It'll make people think you're having more fun than they are, and soon enough they'll probably be trying to . . . ahem . . . steal *your* moves!

IF YOU DON'T WANT TO DANCE...

 ### Help out.

You can't dance if you're manning the refreshment stand. So get behind that table and start ladling the punch. Or see if you can help the deejay spin.

 ### Pull out your cell phone.

Talking on the phone is a perfectly good excuse for not being out on the dance floor. If you have someone to call, that's a bonus, but if not, you can simply pretend. If someone comes over and wants you to dance, give him the "just a minute, please" index finger, followed by a point to your phone and then the "chatty mouth" hand gesture. He'll quickly get the idea and leave you alone.

Start a card game.

No one says you have to be dancing to be the center of activity. So bring a few decks of cards and a bag of pretzels, and recruit a few other players for a game. As soon as other kids see what you're up to, they'll want to join in, too.

Smooth Ways to Ask Someone to Dance

Flying solo and dancing with a group of friends are both acceptable options, but if you want to ask someone to dance with you, here are some easy ways to ask.

• "I bet you and I would be the best dancers out there if we gave it a shot."

• "Do you know how to dance?" If the person says "Yes," reply, "I dare you to show me." If the person says "No," respond, "I can teach you!"

• "Would you like to dance?" If the person says "No," say, "I didn't think so. I just didn't want to be rude before asking your friend."

How to Survive an Embarrassing Adult

It's an age-old question: Are embarrassing adults born or made? Hard to say. And they're even harder to handle. There are two basic ways of dealing with embarrassing adults: a tough "right back atcha" method or the gentler "moral high ground" approach.

THE "RIGHT BACK ATCHA" METHOD

 Embarrass them back.

Start speaking in pirate talk by adding "Aaarggh!" and "To the plank with you, matey!" to the end of your sentences. Alternatively, you could pretend you are an alien. Comment on how welcoming the people of this planet have been and say, "You must visit me on Mars sometime. Bring the kids." Soon enough, whatever uncomfortable behavior the adult is doing will stop as she tries to figure out how to make *you* stop embarrassing *her*.

 Become the interrupting cow.

There's an old joke that goes like this:

Me: *Knock, knock.*

You: *Who's there?*

Me: *The interrupting cow.*

You: *The interrupting cow wh—*

Me: *Moooo!*

When your adult starts saying something terrifically embarrassing, interrupt the conversation by mooing at him.

THE "MORAL HIGH GROUND" APPROACH

 Justice is blind and so shall you be.
If said adult does something incredibly awkward (like picks a wedgie or nose, his or someone else's), pretend you have temporarily gone blind and didn't see it. Making the "How could you do that? I'm *so* embarrassed" face will only make the situation worse.

 Ask for a private moment.
Pull the offending adult aside, out of earshot of everyone else. In a calm voice, explain that you feel uncomfortable, and would she please stop doing X? Stress that you know she's not trying to embarrass you, but you're just feeling extra-sensitive today.

 Make an advance plan.
If you'll be with someone who is likely to bring up the most embarrassing thing about you—say, the fact that you used to shove crayons up your nose because you liked the way they smelled—make an agreement that certain topics will not be raised and that comments like "She still misspells her name" will be avoided.

CHAPTER 4

Survival Skills for the Outdoors

How to Walk to School in Nasty Weather

How many times have you heard the old refrain "When I was a kid I had to walk to school in three feet of snow—uphill"? And how many times have you wanted to reply, "Yeah, but that was back in the Ice Age!" If you find you have to head out into the storm yourself, here's how to weather it gracefully.

Gear Up

1 Gear up.

Before stepping outside, kit yourself out in foul-weather gear: ski goggles, expedition-weight parka, hooded raincoat—whatever the weather dictates. Serious gear will prevent you from turning up in class looking like a drowned rat.

2 Make your footwear watertight.

Should your boots be nowhere in sight (or too hideous to wear!), you can prevent your feet from facing water torture. Just follow these steps:

- *Find two small plastic bags that will fit over your shoes.*
- *Put one foot in the center of a bag and pull the bag up around your leg.*
- *Wrap masking tape tightly around the bag just under your knee.*
- *Repeat with other foot.*

BE AWARE • Though plastic-bag booties may look stylish, they're not terribly sturdy. To prevent them from tearing—and yourself from skidding—avoid running while you're wearing them.

3 Use your umbrella as a shield.

Umbrellas aren't just for raindrops falling on your head. When rain and snow are being blown into your face, aim your umbrella slightly forward like a shield, to block the onslaught. Just make sure to peek out from behind the umbrella every so often to see where you're going.

Clever Excuses to Stay Home in Bad Weather

- "You don't want me to melt, do you?"

- "I'm already having a bad hair day. This is just going to push me over the edge, and you don't want to be responsible for that."

- "Since I don't have windshield wipers on my glasses, I won't be able to see where I'm going."

- "All the acid rain could burn holes in the new clothes you bought me."

- "This weather is literally a sign from above that I should stay home today."

How to Survive Outdoor Chores

It's a sunny day. You *should* be playing outside. But someone else—someone clearly too old to remember the definition of the word *fun*—has other plans for you.

RAKING LEAVES

Though they were pretty when they were on the trees, now that they're scattered all over the lawn they're suddenly a problem—*your* problem. But some skillful rake action can clear that right up.

1 Get it straight.

Veteran rake handlers have a secret: They rake in straight lines from the "bottom" of the lawn to the "top" (or vice versa) so it's always clear what section of the yard they've just finished. Random raking can lead to confusion, and chances are you'll wind up doing certain sections twice, which will make your raking time last even longer.

2 Pile it up.

Instead of making one giant pile, rake your leaves into medium-sized to small piles. If the wind is blowing, a big pile runs the risk of being blown all over the lawn. A big pile also increases the likelihood that some jokester will go cannonballing into your hard work.

3 Bag it, man.

Get a large plastic garbage bag and lay it on the ground right near your first pile. Stick your feet in the bag's opening and slide them apart to open the bag wide. Now, with one hand, pick up the top edge of the bag, forming a triangle. With your free hand, start scooping those leaves into that bag.

Rake in straight lines from the "bottom" of the lawn to the "top."

SHOVELING SNOW

Snow days are awesome—until a shovel is put in your hand and you've got to clean up a mess you didn't even make. But think of it this way: Once you've finished shoveling, you can start pelting those who made you do the job with some really primo snowballs.

1 Don't put off till later what you can scoop faster now.

Snow that has just fallen is actually lighter and easier to shovel than snow that's been on the ground for a while. The longer snow stays on the ground, the more likely it is to partially melt and form a solid, heavy mass that's tightly packed and difficult to move.

2 Don the uniform.

Make sure you've got good gloves, waterproof boots, a warm coat, a fuzzy hat, and a big ol' scarf wrapped around your neck before you start (corncob pipe optional). It's important to stay warm while you're shoveling, so bundle up. (You move more slowly when you're cold, so staying warm will help you get the shoveling over more quickly.)

3 Push the mush.

Instead of lifting the snow with your shovel, push it forward. Space your hands out on the shovel's handle—one toward the top, one closer to the bottom—because this increases your leverage. Better leverage makes the job easier. For the same reason, keep the shovel close to your body, too.

BE AWARE • Once you've pushed the snow off the area you're trying to clean, don't throw it over your shoulder. The twisting movement can strain your back muscles.

Push the Mush   Don't Do the Twist

WASHING THE FAMILY CAR

Is there anything sadder than a car window begging, "Wash me"? If a note like this has been etched in the dust of your family's car, grab a bucket, a sponge, and some soap, because it's time to make that ride of yours shine.

1 Make bubbles.

Put your soap in a large (clean) plastic bucket, then fill the bucket with cool or warm water. You might be tempted to use hot water, but that's not good for the finish, so "stay cool" in terms of water temperature.

2 Hose her down.

Remove excess dirt on the surface of the car before you start the real washing process. Spray the car with a hose, starting from the roof and working your way down to wet its whole surface. You don't need to use a lot of water, just enough to get 'er damp. (Note: When spraying, don't use high pressure, because this can scratch the finish.)

3 Suds it up.

Dunk your sponge or wash mitt into the soapy water and swirl it around to distribute the soap in the mixture.

Once your washing device is good and soaped, start cleaning the car from top to bottom, roof to wheels. Hose her down again to remove any traces of soap.

4 Pat that baby dry.

It's a good idea to dry off the car after washing it: If it's driven when wet, dirt particles from the road will stick, and you might have to do the whole job again! Get a few old cotton towels and gently blot the car's surface. Start at the top of the car and be gentle: You don't want to risk hurting the finish of the car you just spent so long trying to make look good!

How to Survive a Canine Encounter

They say dog is man's best friend. But even a best friend can get snappy sometimes, and this one has a sharp set of teeth. Here's how to handle a pooch like a pro.

DON'T TOUCH A HAIR ON HIS HEAD

Be smart about introducing yourself to a dog you don't know.

⭐ **Ask the owner before petting a pup.**
Since all dogs have different personalities, it's important to ask the owner if the dog is friendly. You never know: That innocent-looking pup could have a ferocious bite.

⭐ **Say yes to sniffing.**
One of the ways a dog gets to know people is by sniffing them. So if your new four-legged friend starts nosing up to you, don't be scared, just hold the back of your hand out to him so he can catch your scent.

Say Yes to Sniffing

 Pet under the chin or on the chest.

Once you've gotten permission from the dog's owner, you should first stroke the dog on her chin or chest so she can keep an eye on your hands. If you pat the top of her head, she might think you're about to hit her!

 Step away from the bone.

Leave her alone when she's eating or chewing on a bone. She might think you're trying to take away her supper.

FOUR LEGS BEAT TWO EVERY TIME

If you're scared a dog might start chasing you and the owner isn't in sight, keep it cool.

1 Don't start a race you can't win.

If you start running, you will only excite the dog's chase instinct. Don't jump up and down, either.

2 Chill out.

Dogs are very sensitive creatures. If you freak out, that will probably cause the animal to do the same thing. If you want the dog to be peaceful, establish a peaceful mindset yourself. Hum your favorite song, dream about your favorite flavor of ice cream—whatever helps you get into a mellow mood.

3 Avoid eye contact and walk away slowly.

Once you've established the peace, you can slip away from the dog slowly and quietly (no sudden jerky movements). Looking into a dog's eyes is considered (by dogs, at least) to be an act of aggression. Avoid the temptation, or the dog may misunderstand you and think you want to fight rather than flee.

How to Deal with Poo on Your Shoe

You really stepped in it this time...and boy, does it stink! So many people hate getting poo on their shoes that many cities have passed "Pooper Scooper" laws, forcing owners to clean up after their pooches. But those laws don't help once you've gone skidding through a patch of poo. Here's how to make this humiliating situation a little less stinky.

1 Do the "scrape, scrape, twist."

To get the top layer of poo off your shoe, find the nearest curb and scrape your shoe—from heel to toe—against it. Repeat. Step in a shallow puddle if you can find one. Now locate a clean patch of sidewalk or grass and twist your foot around in it to loosen the deeper levels of doo in your shoe.

2 Use a sole shovel.

Take the sharp end of the stick or the blunt point of a pencil and begin digging it through the grooves in your sole. Pause to wipe it on the ground or on a piece of paper that you'll throw out later.

3 Give your shoe a once-over with a damp paper towel.

4 Check for skid marks.

Drag the shoe across a dry paper towel as a test. If the paper towel is skid-mark free, your work is done. If your shoe leaves a trail, repeat step 3 and test again.

5 Wash your hands post-poo removal!

How to Deal with Things That Sting

Okay, so your neighborhood isn't exactly the Amazon rain forest. But that doesn't mean there aren't plenty of dangerous creatures lurking around out there. These tips aren't 100 percent insect proof, but they'll keep you as stinger free as possible. You can use them to deal with bees, mosquitoes, wasps, horseflies, and any other pesky stinging insects.

★ **Skip the perfume when you're outdoors.**
Insects are attracted to strong odors. If you know you'll be spending a lot of time outside, avoid using perfume, cologne, or even really smelly soaps.

★ **Avoid tiptoeing through the clover barefoot.**
How much would it stink—and hurt!—to get stung between your toes? A lot. But a bee can't tickle your tootsies if you're wearing shoes. So for feet's sake, put on your footgear.

Avoid dusk and dawn.

Mosquitoes are most active at these times of day. And avoiding dawn is yet another good excuse to sleep in!

 Don't wear brightly colored clothing.

Many insects respond to bright, wild colors and patterns (they think you're a flower), so put that vivid yellow shirt away for the day.

The SWAT Team

The best way to swat a fly or a mosquito is to use two hands. Although those little buggers might see one hand coming at them, their brains are too tiny to figure out what to do once a second hand appears. When you see a fly, slowly move your hands around both sides of its body. It will be so bewildered that you should be able to swat it simply by clapping your hands.

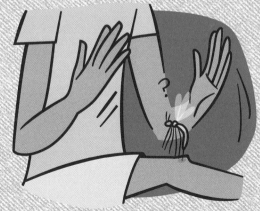

How Not to Avoid Bees

 Stay calm. Repeat: Stay calm.

If a bee lands on you, it will almost always leave on its own. It's just like a dog that wants to sniff you. If you start flapping your arms or shrieking, you risk making it defensive, which is when it's most likely to sting. If you can't wait for the bee to leave on its own, gently and slowly brush it away with a piece of paper.

IF STUNG...

Try to put mind over matter and convince yourself that you're not *really* crazy itchy. But if that doesn't work, give these suggestions a whirl.

> **BE AWARE** • If you start hyperventilating or having a hard time breathing, or if the stung area starts swelling like crazy, find an adult—or have a friend find one—*immediately*. You could be having a dangerous allergic reaction.

★ Ice it.

Numb the bite with an ice pack or ice wrapped in a towel.

★ Paste it.

Combine baking soda and just enough water to make a sticky paste and dab it onto your bite. Or, you can squeeze a little toothpaste onto the itchy area. Both pastes help dry out and shrink the bite.

★ Soap it.

Sometimes rubbing the itch with a bar of soap helps soothe the spot.

Whatever you do, don't scratch it.
You'll wind up making the itch worse, not better. If you must scratch, use your knuckles, since germs under your nails could cause an infection.

Unsavory Plants to Avoid

Insects aren't the only stingers in the wilderness. If you encounter either of these ghastly green growths, steer clear!

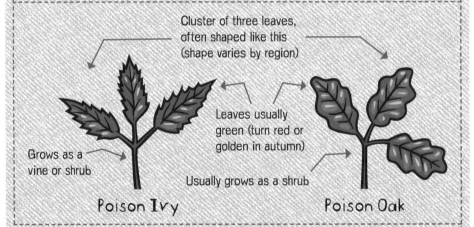

Cluster of three leaves, often shaped like this (shape varies by region)

Leaves usually green (turn red or golden in autumn)

Grows as a vine or shrub

Usually grows as a shrub

Poison Ivy

Poison Oak

If you *do* happen to touch one of these plants, act fast! Get an adult's help to clean your skin with rubbing alcohol or special soap designed to remove the itch-causing plant oils. Use plenty and rinse with lots of cool water—this is no time for moderation!

How to Handle a Bicycle Misadventure

Wearing a helmet, using reflectors, and riding with care are the best ways to stay safe on your bike. But if you and your ride hit a rough patch, here's what to do.

SLIPPED CHAIN

You shift gears and suddenly the pedals lock up or you have zero resistance. What's up? Your chain has jumped the rails.

1 Turn your bike upside down.

To stabilize your bike, turn it upside down so it's standing on its seat and handlebars.

2 Catch the teeth.

Using your fingers or a stick, lift the chain and place it onto the teeth in the rear chain ring, and then onto the teeth in the front chain ring. The chain won't fit all the way around—it'll just hang loosely from the front ring.

Lift the chain and place it onto the teeth.

Catch the Teeth

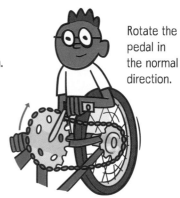

Rotate the pedal in the normal direction.

Rotate and Roll

3 Rotate and roll.

Keeping your fingers out of reach of the chain, grab the nearest pedal and rotate it very slowly in the normal pedaling direction. The chain should thread its way back on.

When You Need a Bike Doctor

Things went seriously wrong, and you (and your bike) went down. After you've picked yourself up and brushed off the dirt (you *were* wearing your helmet, right?), assess your bike. If you have any of the following issues, it's best to leave repairs to the pros:

- Bent frame or front fork
- Flat tire
- Broken chain
- Snapped brake cable

SLIPPERY ROADS

Slick roads are a bicyclist's nightmare. The best solution is to avoid riding in the rain at all. But if your sunny day ends in puddles and spray, here's what to do.

1 Survey the territory.

It takes a lot longer to stop when it's wet. Plus, roads are more slippery after a little rain, because the water mixes with surface oils. Be on the lookout for super-slick manhole covers, oily patches (look for rainbows), and fallen leaves.

2 Give it a brake.

Wet brakes take much longer to stop a bike, so test your brakes before you need to use them. Take it slow, and don't wait until you're flying out of control to start braking.

BE AWARE • On wet roads, back-pedal gently or apply light pressure to your brakes—braking suddenly could cause you to skid.

③ Keep your turns wide.

A tight turn (or a swerve) on a slippery road ups your chances of spinning out. If you start to skid, reduce pressure on the brakes a little.

④ Lighten up.

Falling rain or spray from cars can make visibility poor for drivers. In these conditions, it's really important to wear bright clothing and have reflectors on your bike.

⑤ Walk it off.

If you're facing a steep downhill or pouring rain, remember that there's no shame in walking your bike!

Beware:
Slick roads=slick brakes

How to Survive Getting Lost in the Woods

Your family thought it would be a great idea to "get back to nature" and take a hike in the woods. Unfortunately, some of them have such a bad sense of direction they'd have trouble finding their way out of a paper bag! If those in charge have led you astray (a.k.a. gotten you lost), stay calm and suggest the following ideas.

1 ## Stop and re-step.

Once you realize you've wandered off the trail, go no farther. Retrace your footsteps to get back to the trail. Do *not* be tempted to take a shortcut—this can get you even more lost. Look for blazes (splotches of paint on trees) or cairns (rock piles)—these signs indicate the direction of the trail.

2 ## Don't panic.

Even if you're afraid you're really, really lost, a cool head will help you find your way home faster than a frantic one.

Prepare, Prepare, Prepare

The best way to avoid getting lost in the first place is to do some careful planning before you head into the woods. Make sure the adults you're hiking with have told someone at home where you are heading and are equipped with the following essentials.

- Map, plus guidebook or trail description

- Extra clothing: extra warm layers and a waterproof layer

- Extra water: at least 2–3 quarts (2–3 L) per person per day

- Water filter or treatment pellets

- Reliable fire starter (like waterproof matches)

- Food for the day (plus extra for an emergency)

- Whistle

- Sunscreen

- Insect repellent

- First-aid kit

This may sound like a lot of gear for a short day hike, and you will probably never need some of it. But if you *do* need it, you'll be very glad you have it!

Stick together.

You may be mad that your folks got you lost, but you don't want to make the situation worse by losing them, too. Stick close to your fellow hikers. The more of you there are, the better chance you'll have of attracting help.

Make sure you are equipped with essentials, including but not limited to: a map, extra layers (warm and waterproof), and extra water.

Thar she blows!

Make signals to help people locate you. Give your whistle three long toots, then wait and toot three times again in another direction. (If you forgot your whistle, just shout, "Help!") If someone calls back to you, wait for *them* to come to *you* and lead you back to the trail.

5 Hug a tree.

If help *doesn't* come right away, it's important to stay put. Wandering around off the trail could get you even more lost, or worse, injured. Find a warm, safe, visible spot and stay there.

6 Bundle up and take care of yourselves.

The key things you need to survive are water, warmth, and food. It's a lot harder to warm yourself once you've gotten cold, so put on your extra layers to retain your body heat. You wisely prepared your backpacks with emergency supplies before you left home (*didn't you?*), so now's the time to use them. Drink to stay hydrated, and eat your trail mix to stay nourished. And since you told people where you were headed and when you'd be back (*right?*), help should eventually come.

7 Graciously accept thanks.

Your companions will be *very* glad you made sure they were prepared. No need to say, "I told you so" (at least until you get safely home).

Appendix

USEFUL SCHOOLYARD COMEBACKS

The best tool to carry into the schoolyard is a sharp mind. The best comebacks make a person scratch his head as he tries to think of something smart to say back to *you*.

- "I never forget a face. But in your case I'll make an exception."

- "You can say whatever you want to me and I won't get mad—it's Be Kind to Animals Week."

- "I'm not upset by what you said. I know you did it without thinking . . . just like you do everything else."

- "If I agreed with you, we'd both be wrong."

- "I don't know what your problem is, but I bet it's hard to pronounce."

- "You may be trying to insult me, but I know you like me. I can see your tail wagging."

- "I really want to help you out. Which way did you come in?"

HANDY EXCUSES FOR NOT HANDING IN YOUR HOMEWORK

Here's our best advice: Do your homework. Here's our best advice if you didn't follow *that* advice: Use one of these lines.

- "I didn't do it because I didn't want to add to your workload."

- "I thought you said it was due tomorrow, and since today is *today*, I'll bring it tomorrow."

- "You'll be happy to know I told myself, 'Self, do your homework!' Unfortunately, actions speak louder than words."

- "I did my homework, but aliens took it to study how the human brain works."

- "It's true, I didn't do my homework. But since I want to impress you, I'll do it right away."

- "The truth is, I was too tired to do my homework last night. But a good night's sleep fixed all that."

- "My head told me to do it, but my hand had the final say."

- "I'm sorry I don't have my homework. My underpants were too tight, and they cut off the circulation to my brain."

CONTRACT WITH NOSY BROTHER OR SISTER RE: "STAYING OUT OF MY STUFF"

To Whom It May Concern:

I, brother/sister of _____ , do hereby state that I understand that I
              (your name)
am hereby banned from snooping in _____'s room. Furthermore,
                        (your name)
I will (a) keep my paws to myself, (b) not put my nose where it does
not belong, and (c) prevent my eyeballs from "accidentally" looking
at his/her personal, private, and confidential stuff.

If I am caught breaking any of these rules, I will voluntarily hand over
my favorite toy, _____. My brother/sister will get to
                (favorite toy name)
keep this toy for at least one day while I think about my crime of
snooping and why it was oh-so-wrong.

Signed,

_____
(Signature of sibling. If sibling is too young to
sign name, marking an "X" is acceptable.)

                                _____
                                (Date)

Witnessed by:

_____
(Signature of witness)

                                _____
                                (Date)

CONTRACT WITH KID BROTHER OR SISTER RE: "HANG TIME"

To Whom It May Concern:

I, little brother/sister of _____, do hereby state that I understand the "One Time Only" rule of hanging out with _____.
(your name)

To be clear, the "One Time Only" rule means that just because an adult
has encouraged my fantastic older brother/sister to spend time with me
today, I totally get that it doesn't mean he/she will be doing so tomorrow.

Furthermore, I agree to try my hardest to be as little a pest as possible
when we're hanging out. This means I will do my best not to annoy,
embarrass, humiliate, anger, poke, prod, or sneeze on or near my
dear sibling. I will honor his/her requests not to lag behind. I will
bring him/her snacks when asked. I will keep quiet when asked. And
I will never tell anyone his/her embarrassing middle name.

Signed,

_____   _____
(Signature of sibling. If sibling is too young to   (Date)
sign name, marking an "X" is acceptable.)

Witnessed by:

_____   _____
(Signature of witness)   (Date)

About the Authors

David Borgenicht is a writer, editor, publisher, and the coauthor of all the books in the Worst-Case Scenario Survival Handbook series. He has survived dozens of childhood nightmares, including the one where you wake up naked in the middle of a test you haven't studied for. He now lives a stable adult life in Philadelphia.

As a child, **Robin Epstein** never met a worst-case scenario she didn't take on headfirst (and she has the scar on her forehead to prove it). She credits her parents for nurturing her free spirit and paying her medical bills, and she thanks them for always encouraging her to think critically and use her noggin. She lives in New York City, where her noggin comes in handy every day.

About the Illustrator

Chuck Gonzales is a New York City–based illustrator who was raised in South Dakota. His work often blends his suburban upbringing and his present urban existence. His client base has been just as diverse, including the *New York Times*, the *Washington Post*, Disney, Nickelodeon, Nick Jr., and Chronicle Books. Growing up in the Dakotas as a short, artsy, neurotic kid, he was not spared any junior high indignities.

The
WORST-CASE SCENARIO
Survival Handbook:

EXTREME

Junior Edition

The
WORST-CASE SCENARIO
Survival Handbook:
EXTREME
Junior Edition

By David Borgenicht and Justin Heimberg

Illustrated by Chuck Gonzales

chronicle books · san francisco

A WORD OF WARNING: It's always important to keep safety in mind. If you're careless, even the tamest activities can result in injury. As such, all readers are urged to act with caution, ask for adult advice, obey all laws, and respect the rights of others when handling any Worst-Case Scenario.

Worst-Case Scenario and The Worst-Case Scenario Survival Handbook are trademarks of Quirk Productions, Inc.

Book design by Lynne Yeamans.
Typeset in Adobe Garamond, Blockhead, and Imperfect.
Illustrations by Chuck Gonzales.

Library of Congress Cataloging-in-Publication Data
Borgenicht, David.
  The worst-case scenario survival handbook : extreme junior edition / by David Borgenicht and Justin Heimberg ; Illustrated by Chuck Gonzales.
    p. cm.
  ISBN 978-0-8118-6568-5
  1. Social skills in children—Juvenile literature. 2. Socialization—Juvenile literature. 3. Children—Humor—Juvenile literature. I. Heimberg, Justin. II. Gonzales, Chuck. III. Title.
  HQ783.B663 2008
  613.6'9—dc22
  2008014580

Manufactured by Toppan Leefung, Da Ling Shan Town, Dongguan, China, in June 2010.

10 9 8 7 6 5

This product conforms to CPSIA 2008.

Chronicle Books LLC
680 Second Street, San Francisco, California 94107

www.chroniclekids.com

CONTENTS

Welcome to Team Extreme

You may have heard the saying "If life hands you lemons, make lemonade." That's great, but what do you do when those lemons are being handed to you by a 400-pound (181-kg) gorilla? This guide will prepare you for just that sort of scenario, and it'll give you hundreds of other tips to help you become the ultimate extreme adventurer.

And when we say extreme, we mean *EXTREME!* In capital letters. And italics. With an exclamation point. Yes, the first day of school is *extremely* uncomfortable, and a wedgie from a bully can be *extremely* painful. But we're talking about a whole different level of *extreme*. We're talking pythons, tarantulas, sandstorms, piranhas, sharks, quicksand, elephant stampedes, mountain lions, tigers, and bears, oh my!

When faced with these kinds of extreme situations, extreme action must be taken. FAST! There's no time to sit down and draw a flow chart. No time to phone a friend or ask your parents for advice. It's all about *you*, and what *you* know, right then, right away.

But don't freak out. The information in this book spans the globe, across the seven continents, from ocean to desert to forest to tundra. No unsafe place is safe from our extreme survival know-how. So whether you're going on an adventure in Africa, the Arctic, or merely in your imagination, you're covered. Just stay calm. Surviving an extreme worst-case scenario is as easy as 1, 2, 3 . . . (OK, sometimes you might need 4, 5, 6.)

But even if you don't have plans to go on safari or explore the tundra any time soon, you'll still find this book packed with interesting (and sometimes surprising!) facts. Did you know, for example, that the most dangerous animal in Africa is actually the mosquito? Or that lightning really *can* strike the same place twice? And did you know that tarantulas can shoot their hairs like tiny darts? You *will* know after you read this guide.

Read, and dare we say, study up. Commit these tips to memory, because a good extreme adventurer is an informed extreme adventurer.

So turn the page and begin your initiation into Team Extreme. When you're done reading, you'll have everything you need to take on the world's worst (not to mention lots of cool information to impress your friends with). Good luck on your journeys.

Be safe. Be smart. Be extreme.

—David Borgenicht and Justin Heimberg

CHAPTER 1

How to Survive at Sea

How to Fend Off a Shark

Few images spark as much fear in swimmers as a shark fin slicing through the water. Never mind that deer kill 300 times more people a year than sharks! (See *Oh Deer!*, page 38.) But even though shark attacks are *very* rare, it's good to know what to do if Jaws drops in on your swim.

1 Stay calm.

This is sort of a given. It wouldn't be very good advice to tell you to panic and scream like a baby, would it? The point is, just because you see a shark does not mean it will attack. Signs a shark may be getting just a little deadly include it swimming in increasingly smaller circles and rubbing its belly against the seafloor.

2 Hit it!

If a shark comes at you, you have just one choice: Fight back. Fight dirty. Go for the shark's most sensitive spots: its eyes and gill openings. Punch, poke, and kick. This is a pro-wrestling match, and you're the bad guy.

3 A boxer never quits.

Keep on hitting the shark—jab it over and over in its sensitive spots. If you can convince your toothy opponent you're too much trouble, it may look elsewhere for its lunch. After all, you wouldn't want to eat a peanut butter and jelly sandwich that slapped you across the face, would you?

4 Get away.

Your best bet is to get on dry land, where Jaws can't follow (at least not before another million years of evolution). If you're in too deep (like if you're scuba diving), try hiding in weeds or against the seafloor, where it'll be harder for the shark to get to you.

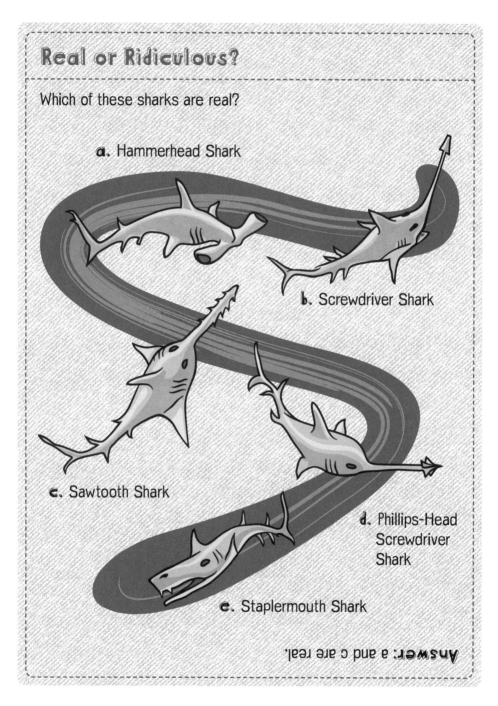

Real or Ridiculous?

Which of these sharks are real?

a. Hammerhead Shark

b. Screwdriver Shark

c. Sawtooth Shark

d. Phillips-Head Screwdriver Shark

e. Staplermouth Shark

Answer: a and c are real.

How to Build a Raft After a Shipwreck

At first, the idea of being shipwrecked on a remote island seems pretty cool—endless days frolicking on the beach. Then again, there's no air conditioning or video games. Here's how to get back to the real world.

1 Go logging.
Clear a path into the interior of the island and find two logs about your height and ten logs about twice your height. OK, lumberjack, now lug those babies back toward the shore. Hey, no one said this was going to be easy.

2 Live on the edge.
Place the two short logs at the edge of the water at low tide. This is important: You wouldn't want to build the world's greatest raft, complete with swimming pool and mini golf, only to realize you can't get it in the water. Lay the longer logs on top of and across the shorter ones so they extend a bit past both short logs.

❸ The rest is easy—*knot*!

Here's the hard part. You need to tie the logs together. Seaweed or vines are probably your best bet for string substitutes if you don't have actual string. Securely tie the logs together with long lengths of vine wrapped in figure eights and as many knots as you can.

❹ Surf's up, ship out.

When the tide comes in, the water will flow under and around the raft. The raft will start to float, and you can push it out into the water. Now all you need to do is survive in the world's biggest wave pool (see *How to Survive When You're Adrift at Sea*, page 18). Good luck!

Island Inventions
(in Decreasing Order of Genius)

Surviving is all about being resourceful and creative. What would *you* make if you were stranded on a deserted island?

Tepee using logs and parachute

Shiny coin fishing lure and thorn hook

Palm leaf water collector

Coconut basketball

Flounder hat

How to Survive When You're Adrift at Sea

If you're ever in a shipwreck, you'll need your wits, your strength, and your nerves of steel. Oh, and a lifeboat would help! Once you're adrift in the great deep blue, use these tips to steer yourself to safety.

1 Collect rainwater.

Supply your boat or raft with things that can function as containers: bottles, hollow coconuts, your World's Greatest Grandkid mug, anything. Let them sit in the rain to collect water. Then put lids on your containers (you can make lids out of whatever is handy) so you can store the water and avoid spills. Drink small sips, not big gulps, so your body can absorb the water.

2 No loose ends.

Tie your water containers to you or the boat to make sure you don't lose them. In fact, you may want to tie *yourself* to the boat so you don't lose *you*.

3 Don't work on your tan.

Act like a vampire at the beach and cover your skin as much as possible to avoid sunburn and sunstroke.

4 Land ho!

If you're in a busy area, you might be found by another ship. If not, keep your eye out for land. Even if you can't see land, there are signs you're nearing it:

- **Birds.** They'll fly back to an island at night, so follow their lead.
- **Driftwood.** If it's floating, land's approaching.
- **Murky water.** Muddy water means a river's mouth may be near—land could be just over the horizon.

5 Shore thing.

Choose a sandy beach over a more dangerous rocky or coral shore. If necessary, drift along the shore until you find the perfect place to land.

What's Your Worst Case?

Being stranded in a sea of snot?

or

Being stranded in a sea of vomit?

How to Avoid a Tsunami

Rearrange the letters in the word *tsunami,* and you can spell "I am nuts," which is what you are if you stay near the ocean when one of these monster waves approaches. Learn the warning signs so you can be far away when the ten-story-high waves come crashing down.

1 Hey, wasn't there an ocean here just now?
If the water level suddenly drops or rises for no clear reason, that's one sign of a coming tsunami. Or maybe a giant sea creature just took a big swallow. Either way, take the water movement as a cue to get your butt out of the water—and away from the beach altogether.

2 Water-quake!
Tsunamis are caused by underwater earthquakes. If you're on the shore and the ground begins to shake or you hear a low continuous roar, it's time to get going. Don't stop to grab your flippers.

3 Up, up, and away.

Get yourself off the beach and up to a high place, like the peak of the local mountain or the top floor of a tall building.

4 Aah—aaah—*tsu*!!

Like sneezes, the waves of a tsunami can keep on coming. Stay high and dry till things calm down. You don't want to end up soaked.

What Would You Do?

You are on a sailboat in a small harbor when you hear a loud roar and the sea level toward the shore seems to have dropped. What should you do?

a. Take your boat far into open water.

b. Stay where you are and lower the sail.

c. Sail near other boats—safety in numbers.

d. Abandon ship and dive to the magical undersea land of Zarnia, where the water nymphs and naiads can protect you.

Answer: a. Take your boat far into open water. Oftentimes, tsunamis are not even felt in deep water.

My Hero!

In 2004, a ten-year-old British girl named Tilly Smith, who had studied tsunamis in geography class, saw the receding ocean on Mai Khao Beach in northern Phuket, Thailand, and became a hero. She and her parents warned others on the beach, which was evacuated safely.

How to Treat a Jellyfish Sting

Imagine a mop made of stingers brushing across your body, and you'll have an idea of what it feels like to get stung by a jellyfish. The good news is that with the right recipe, you can at least lessen the zing of that sting.

1 Please pass the *salt*water.

Freshwater's the way to go when brushing your teeth, shampooing, and just about everything else. But with

a jellyfish sting, freshwater will actually make the sting feel worse, because it washes away salts that help lessen the sting. Rinse the sting with seawater.

2 Break out the vinegar.

White vinegar, to be more specific. Why treat your wound like a salad? Because of *nematocysts*. Nematocysts are tiny structures in the cells of jellyfish that deliver the sting by firing tiny "darts" of venom. The acid in the vinegar deactivates these beasts. Bottom line: The vinegar takes the sting out. (No need to add croutons.)

3 Remove any tentacles.

Lift, don't scrape, any tentacles off using a stick or glove. If you scrape them off, you'll cause more stings to occur. You already have an entire Braille alphabet of stings on you, so there's no need for more.

4 To pee or not to pee? That is the question.

Some say *peeing* on a jellyfish sting will ease the pain. However, an Australian study showed that it actually caused more, not less, firing of nematocysts. So, it's best not to pee on yourself or a friend. What a relief!

How to Navigate by the Stars

Centuries ago, sailors used the stars to keep their ships on course at night. And guess what? Those stars are still twinkling, so you can use them to figure out which way is which, whether you're at sea or on land.

1 **Take a dip.**

The North Star (also known as Polaris) isn't the brightest star, so we use other stars to locate it, like the stars of the Big Dipper. You can't miss the Big Dipper—it looks like a big ladle that's scooping up some star soup.

2 **Use your pointers.**

Focus on the two stars that form the far end of the ladle's cup. These stars are called "pointers" because they point to the North Star. Just draw an imaginary line through the pointer stars and out across the sky, as shown on the right. The next star you'll see is the North Star.

③ Catch a falling North Star.

OK, stargazer. You've found the North Star. Now imagine that the North Star fell straight to the ground. Go find that fallen star. That's where North is. Now you can figure out south, east, and west—and head in the direction you want to go!

BE AWARE • If you're in the Southern Hemisphere, you can navigate by finding the Southern Cross, which is in the southern part of the sky. Either that, or just turn this page upside down and hope for the best.

Note: The Big Dipper might look like this, or it could be upside down in the sky. Look for it both ways!

Real or Ridiculous?

Which of these constellations are real?

a. Canes Venatici (Hunting Dogs)
b. Ursa Major (The Great Bear)
c. Pantus Cleanus (The Clean Slacks)
d. Castoris Bloatus (The Bloated Beaver)
e. Piscis Austrinus (The Southern Fish)

Answer: a, b, and e are real. Note: The big Dipper is actually a part of the constellation Ursa Major. Can you spot it in the tail?

CHAPTER 2

How to Survive in the Mountains

How to Survive an Erupting Volcano

A volcanic eruption is basically a mountain throwing up. Things have been gurgling around inside for a while, and suddenly—SPEW!—a mess of liquid, solids, and gas is vomited out in a fiery mess. And this stuff really burns. Here's how to make sure that spew doesn't get on yew.

1 Look out—it's raining rocks.

When you think of an erupting volcano, you picture red hot lava flows dripping off a mountain like melting ice cream. But along with the rivers of fire, there are rocks being spit high into the air. If you're anywhere near a mountain that's blowing chunks, take cover if you can, and roll into a ball to protect your head.

Cool Volcano Words

aa (ah-ah): That is not a typo. And it's not you screaming either. *Aa* is a Hawaiian word for a type of lava with a rough surface of hard lava fragments.

caldera (call-DARE-uh): The crater formed by a volcanic explosion. (The mouth of the vomiting volcano.)

kipuka (kip-OOK-uh): A Hawaiian word for an area (like a hill) surrounded by lava flow, like an island in a sea of lava.

magma: Molten rock that is underground.

pillow lava: Blob-shaped formations of cooled lava that form when a lava flow enters the water.

2 Head for the hills!

Oh wait, the hills are on fire. That's not such a good idea. If the lava is headed your way, get out of its path as fast as you can. If you can put a ditch—or better yet, an entire valley—between you and the flow, so much the better.

3 Get inside.

Boiling lava on the ground, rocks raining from the sky? Time to seek shelter. Get inside—anywhere will do—as fast as you can, and try to get to a high story. Close all doors and windows. Don't open the door, not even if the lava knocks politely.

4 Up, up, and away.

Another nasty thing about a volcanic eruption is the mix of deadly gases that are belched forth. Carbon dioxide gas is the worst of 'em, and because it is denser than air, it will collect near the ground, so start climbing—stairs, furniture, whatever will keep your head above the murk.

How to Survive an Avalanche

Imagine being hit by a snowball as big as an ocean liner. That's what it feels like to be in an avalanche, and it's clearly a fight you want to avoid. But if Mother Nature throws the first snowball, staying on top of it (literally) is your best shot at riding to safety.

1 Brace yourself for impact.

If an avalanche is heading your way, don't let your jaw drop in shock—keep your mouth closed tight so you won't choke on snow. If you have ski poles, drop them (they can be dragged away, pulling you down), and crouch behind a tree or find shelter ASAP.

2 Ride the wave.

As the avalanche starts to close in around you, stay on top of the sliding snow by swimming in a freestyle (crawl) motion, using your arms and legs to keep you on the surface. It's the ultimate in bodysurfing.

> **BE AWARE** • Never hike alone in avalanche country, and always carry an emergency beacon—a signaling device that will help rescuers find you if you are buried under snow.

3 **When in doubt, spit.**

If you end up in the middle of a snow cone, you need to find the surface. If you can't tell which end is up, dig a hole around you and spit. Your loogie will head downhill and give you an idea which way is up. Cool, huh?

4 **Dig up.**

Dig toward open air. Dig quickly, or someone may discover you in 2,000 years in the ice and say, "Wow, look at that perfectly preserved expression of panic!"

Avalanches to Imagine

Which kind of avalanche would you *least* like to be in?

- Soccer balls
- Pudding
- Fingernail clippings
- Thumbtacks
- Donuts
- Belly button lint
- Spray cheese
- Marbles
- Worms

How to Avoid a Bear Attack

For the most part, bears just want to live an easy country life. However, in certain situations, they can get testy. Like when they're protecting their cubs, feasting on deer, or when their houses have been broken into and vandalized by little blond girls who eat their porridge. Here's how to show bears the respect they deserve.

1 Sing out loud, sing out strong.

You don't want to freak out a bear by surprising it. As you hike, make noise by talking, singing a little forest karaoke, or by having a fascinating conversation with your echo. You could also fasten bells to your shoes or hat. Any sound will clue the bear in that you're coming, so *it* can choose to avoid *you*. That's the best-case scenario!

2 Keep your distance.

If you spot a bear, hold very still, and wait for the bear to go on its merry way. If you can, back away s-l-o-w-l-y to get more distance from the bear.

3 Know who you're dealing with.

Check if the bear is black or brown. Black bears are the most common in North America, but if you're in western North America, you might encounter a brown bear (like the grizzly or Kodiak). Coat colors can vary, though, so if you hike in a region with both black and brown bears, learn all the ways to tell the difference before you head out.

4 Play tricks.

If the bear is a black bear, and it's starting to charge you from afar, wave your arms and make noise—the bear will think you're bigger than you are and will back off. If it's a brown bear, curl up and lie still—playing dead will hopefully cause the bear to lose interest.

Oh Deer!

The most dangerous animal in America? The deer. That's right. Cute little Bambi is responsible for around 1.5 million car collisions in the Unites States alone every year, according to the Insurance Institute for Highway Safety. A total of 150 of these crashes are fatal for humans, and the horns-meeting-headlights destruction causes more than one billion dollars in property damage annually.

But the road isn't the only place a deer can be dangerous. As our neighborhoods start to take over the deer's homes, deer are losing their natural fear of people. During mating season (November–December), there have been an increasing number of deer attacks on humans by rambunctious bucks. With sharp antlers and club-like hooves, deer can be vicious.

Tell your parents to use the follow-ing tips when driving in deer country:

- Pay attention to deer-crossing signs and drive slowly when you see them.
- Be aware that deer are most active between the hours of 6 and 9 p.m.
- Do not attempt to sing a duet with a deer or any other woodland creature.

How to Survive a Lightning Storm on a Mountainside

Have you seen those "storm chasers" on TV? Those crazy folks who drive into the eyes of hurricanes? Do *not* try that at home! But even if you're not chasing storms, sometimes *they'll* chase *you*. Here's how to win this game of tag.

1 Stormwatch.

You love nature—if there are a few black clouds overhead, a little torrential downpour, so what? Lightning, however, is a different story, and you need to be aware of the signs when a storm is so close, you could be stuck:

- **A buzzing sound.** This is the sound of static electricity caused by tiny particles called electrons dancing about.
- **A sudden gravity-defying change in your hairstyle.** Your new 'do is the result of electricity in the air and in your hair!
- **A halo of light around people or trees.** No, you're not seeing things—well, actually you are,

but it's a real phenomenon known as "St. Elmo's Fire." The high voltage in the air reacts with the gas around objects and people to create the glow. Pretty cool.

2 **Do the math.**

Arithmetic may be the last thing on your mind at a time like this, but a little division can help you figure out how close to you the storm is. When you see lightning, count the number of seconds until you hear thunder. Then divide by five. That's how far away the storm is in miles. Get to a safe place immediately if the thunder snaps,

crackles, or pops less than 30 seconds after the lightning. A storm even 6 miles away is within lightning-strike range. (It doesn't have to be raining on you for lightning to find you!)

③ Heavy metal?
Take off backpacks with metal frames and any jewelry. That navel piercing makes your belly button a bull's-eye. Tall things and metal objects are what lightning likes. That's why telephone poles aren't good hiking buddies.

Real or Ridiculous?

Which of the following are *real* effects of being struck by lightning? Which are *ridiculous*?

- You can turn the lights on and off by blinking.
- Your popcorn starts to pop before you put the bag in the microwave.
- Your hair is dark and curly (but it used to be blond and straight).
- You now sneeze the sound of thunder.
- You have a magnetic personality (literally).

Answer: Of course, *all* of these are ridiculous!

4 Gimme shelter (the right kind).

If you're in the forest and there are trees all around you, choose the shortest one and crouch under it, so you're the shortest thing in the area. If a tree has a lightning scar (usually a vertical patch that's been cut out of the tree or is covered in new, lighter bark), stay away—lightning *can* actually strike the same place twice. Stay away from isolated trees, metal fences, and bodies of water. All of these can attract lightning strikes.

How to Escape from a Mountain Lion

Ah, the peaceful sounds of the mountainside—birds calling, the wind in the trees, the low growl of a mountain lion—uh-oh. Here's how to stay safe in cougar country.

1 **Don't be a copycat.**

When you're near mountain lions (also called cougars and pumas), don't be a copycat; if you don't do like the big cats do, you'll be less likely to meet one. Don't hike at dusk or dawn (when they're on the prowl). If you see scratch marks on the trees, don't think, "Time to sharpen my fingernails." And definitely don't kill and eat a deer.

2 **Run away? Not today.**

Not to sound like the annoying lifeguard, but upon sighting a mountain lion, please do not run. If you run, it is likely to chase you. It's got four legs to your two. It's a lot faster than you. Don't find out the hard way.

3 Grow up.

You want to appear like a big ferocious animal so the lion doesn't think you're some easy-to-chomp little morsel. Look as big as you can. Stand up straight. Flex those muscles! Wave your arms over your head. Spread out your jacket like a king cobra. Bare your teeth and make some noise, y'all!

4 Back up.

If your tough-guy act doesn't petrify the puma, then you need to make the first move to break up this unhealthy relationship. Standing tall, slowly back away from the mountain lion.

5 Throw up.

This lion is not getting the hint; instead of walking away, he's stalking today. He's looking intently at you and crouching. You need to make it clear that you're not defenseless. Pick up some stones and toss them at the lion. Hard.

6 Protect your neck.

If the lion pounces, do not curl up to protect yourself. Mountain lions like to bite the back of the neck. Stay upright and maneuver to keep your neck away from the lion—kind of like how you'd avoid turning your back to a bully who likes to give wedgies. And yeah, a mountain lion neck bite is a *little* different from a wedgie, but you get the idea!

How to Go to the Bathroom in the Woods

Mountain lions, avalanches, volcanoes—all formidable foes. But what's the #1 wilderness worry? It's going #2.

1 Find your magic spot.

Pick a potty spot behind a tree or rock for privacy, far from the trail. This isn't a spectator sport. Stay at least 100 feet (30 m) away from any water source.

2 Dig a doo ditch.

Use a stick to dig a hole to bury your treasure. Make the hole deep enough to cover your "deposit."

3 Gather materials.

Find some nice soft leaves (unless you brought toilet paper) as wipes. Some hikers use pine cones, dry pine needles, or even a smooth "wiping stone." (Not something you'd want to keep for your rock garden or pet rock collection.)

BE AWARE • You should always make an informed decision on your brand of toilet foliage. Make sure you know what poison ivy looks like!

Poison Ivy

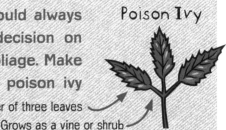

Cluster of three leaves

Grows as a vine or shrub

4 Bury your treasure.

Bury the leaves along with your poo. If you brought toilet paper, carry it out of the woods with you in a sealed plastic bag.

5 Wash your hands.

Wiping in the woods is an art that is rarely perfectly executed. So be sure to wash up. Wet your hands with water from a canteen or use a hand sanitizer.

MAGIC SPOT

The Circle of Life

Everyone has a favorite technique for fertilizing the soil. What's yours?

• The Invisible Chair
Press your back against a tree so your butt is suspended above the ground, as if you were sitting on an imaginary chair.

• The Standard Squat
Take a wide stance and crouch down over your homemade toilet. Note: This is only for those who have good balance.

• The Hanging Squat
Hold on to a tree in front of you, ideally one that bends (but doesn't break!). Place your feet near the base of the tree, bend your knees, and lean back.

• The Fallen Log
Hang your butt over the edge of a fallen log. There are two theories for the origin of the name of this method.

CHAPTER 3

How to Survive in the Desert

How to Get Along with Tarantulas

Relax. It's just a spider. A big hairy spider. With fangs. Fangs that can inject venom. Actually, you *can* relax. A tarantula is not that dangerous. Its venom causes nothing more than some minor swelling (unless you're allergic to it, which is rare). But why get that far?

The Tarantula Twist

1 Play poker.

If a tarantula makes a pit stop on you, find something like a stick or a rolled-up newspaper and gently poke your furry visitor. Poke at it the way you poke your fork at vegetables you don't want to eat. The big guy should mosey on off. Move along fella, nothing to see here.

2 Shake your booty.

If the poking isn't doing the trick, it's time to bounce up and down like an idiot. Stand up, bounce, and shake. So you look a little goofy. The tarantula is not one to judge. Who knows? The Tarantula Twist may become the next big dance craze.

Cool or Scary?

- The Goliath tarantula from South America has a body as big as a Chihuahua.
- Tarantulas actually run after their prey; they don't wait in a web.
- If forced to defend itself, a tarantula may flick tiny barbed hairs from its abdomen at its enemy.

How to Deal with a Scorpion

The scorpion, a relative of spiders, has eight legs and a stinger right at the end of its tail. But a wagging tail doesn't mean a scorpion is happy to see you. Do not lean over it and say, "Oh, wook at dat widdle guy waggin' his widdle tail!" When that stinger-capped tail uncurls like a party blower, the party's over.

1 Play hide and seek.

Comfy hiding spots, such as inside your shoes, under your bed linens, and under your pile of laundry are four-star accommodations to scorpions. Shake out your boots, bed linens, and clothes before using them. And at night, stuff your empty shoes so the scorpions don't tuck themselves in.

2 Leave stones unturned.

Resist turning over rocks or reaching into crevices. If you surprise a scorpion, the next surprise will be on you.

3 No shoes, you lose.

If you're camping in the desert, and you need to go to the bathroom at night, take the time to shake out and put on your shoes before venturing out. Scorpions are nocturnal (meaning they're active at night), and they will sting bare feet if they come their way.

> **BE AWARE •** On rare occasions, scorpions can be born with two tails. Double the pleasure!

How to Protect Yourself in a Sandstorm

Sandstorms can strike quickly and with little warning. One moment you're strolling along the dunes, enjoying the scenery, and the next, you're being blasted by a blizzard of sand grains. Here's how to ride out the storm.

1 Seal your lips.

The first thing to do is to cover your nose and mouth. Wet a bandanna, and, doing your best bandit imitation, wrap it around your face and nose. Resist the temptation to rob a train.

2 Don't stare.

Ever have something caught in your eye, like a gnat? It's torture. In a sandstorm, it's cool to be a four-eyes. If you have goggles or sunglasses, put them on. Turn your head away from the wind and close your eyes.

3 Back that act up.

Turn away from the wind. If you need to move toward the wind—say, back to your car or shelter—walk backward.

Super Sandstorms

Some of the biggest sandstorms in the world occur in the Sahara Desert of Africa, where they're called *haboobs*—Arabic for "strong wind." And "strong wind" is right! Gusts can create walls of sand 3,000 feet high—*twice* as tall as the Empire State Building!

How to Survive an Encounter with a Rattlesnake

Rattlesnakes, like all snakes, are cold-blooded and prefer hot climates. Not surprisingly, these venomous vipers, along with many other scary slitherers, call the desert home. Here's how to keep your cool if a rattler crosses your path.

1 Name that tune.

So, you're hiking a desert trail through the dunes when suddenly you find a large brown snake. You can check your field guide for a snake with a flat triangular head, thick body, and fangs like retractable needles. Or you can take your cue from the rattle at the end of its tail, which will probably start shaking and clacking. It's got a rattle, and it's a snake. Chances are you know what it is already.

> **BE AWARE** • Always stay on clear paths, so you can see what's underfoot!

2 Don't get rattled.

So the rattler is still and coiled up, with a tail that sounds like it's playing the maracas. What does that rattling mean? Rattlesnakes don't come with warning labels, but if they did, this is what they'd say: Warning—if the snake is coiled and head is raised, get out of striking range. Also, if the rattle is a rockin', don't come a knockin'.

3 Freeze!

Don't move. Don't throw stones at the snake or poke it with a stick. Just back away. Give the rattler plenty of room—its striking distance can be half its overall length.

4 Fang you very much.

If you are bitten, stay calm, walk (don't run) to get medical help, and keep the bite above your heart if possible. Do not try to treat the bite yourself by bandaging it or putting anything on it—leave the rescue to the professionals. Though painful, rattler bites are rarely fatal.

Nanny, Nanny Boo-Boo!

Why does a snake stick out its tongue and hiss?

a. It's a warning to would-be attackers.

b. It thinks it's funny to taunt you.

c. It's feeding off particles in the air.

d. It uses its tongue to smell.

Answer: d. The forked tongue picks up odors from the air and touches them to openings in the snake's mouth. This is how a snake smells!

How to Find Water in the Desert

Out in the desert, there's no escaping the sun. Keeping hydrated is the only way to battle the constant thirst. When you've emptied your canteen, here's how to find some new, fresh water.

1 Dry stream? **I thought you** said ice cream.

Look for a dry creek bed—even if there is no water flow-ing, there may be some beneath the surface. Use a stick or your hands, and dig into the stream bottom to see if you find moist sand or water pooling. Dirt soup. Yummy.

2 Trust your animal instincts.

Animals need water too. If you follow an animal's tracks or call, you may be heading for the local wildlife water cooler. Of course, before getting a drink, you'll want to scope out the poolside for any predators.

Are Mirages Real?

A mirage is a real phenomenon that can make you think you're seeing a pool of water ahead of you in the desert. The sight you're seeing is absolutely real—you can even take a picture of it! But of course (sadly!), there's no real water there. This kind of mirage happens when the hot ground warms up the air above it, which causes rays of sunlight to bend so much that you actually see an image of the sky on the ground. This image can *look* like water and even *ripple* like water, but don't be fooled—there's not a drop to drink!

3 Show a "can dew" spirit.

Even in the desert, mornings following cold nights result in desert dew. (There's a bad name for a soda, huh?) You can scrape the dew drops off plants into your mouth. Hey, take what you can get.

How to Stop a Runaway Camel

Whether it's got one hump or two, a camel is the perfect desert transport. It can travel long distances with very little water and withstand the scorching desert sun. Though camels are easily trained, they're still prone to getting startled by loud noises and other surprises, so you'd better be prepared in case the one you're riding decides to make a run for it.

HOW TO RIDE A CAMEL

Before you can rein in a runaway, it's important to know how to ride a camel the right way.

1 You scratch its back . . .

It won't break yours. Rake the camel's coat before putting a saddle on. This removes any sticks or burrs that might be a real pain in the hump if stuck under the saddle. Feel free to gossip with the camel as you do its hair.

The Perfect Desert Vehicle

Paint job: A camel's thick coat reflects sunlight and insulates the body from the heat.

Headlights: Long eyelashes and—check this out—*sealable nostrils* help against blowing sand. There are times when we all wish we had sealable nostrils.

Fuel efficiency: A camel's organs and fatty humps allow it to go without water for long periods. Its pee comes out as thick as syrup and its poop is so dry it is used to light fires.

Wheels: Tough feet protect against hot sand.

headlights

paint job

fuel efficiency

wheels

2 "Down, boy!"

It's a bad idea to take a running jump to mount a camel. Instead, trainers have taught camels to learn commands to make them kneel down. The trainer's Secret Word #1 will get the camel to crouch low enough that you can get on the hump.

3 Don't get tossed.

After you utter Secret Word #2 for "up," the camel will stand. But brace yourself! The camel's backside goes up first and fast. Lean back, or you'll get a face full of sand.

4 Gentle reins.

Riders use reins to steer a camel, just like they would with a horse. However, in the camel's case, the reins are attached to a peg in the nose. It's very punk rock. But be gentle. Think of how painful it is to yank a nose hair, and multiply that by ten.

5 Sway with it.

A camel walks differently from a horse—the camel moves both right legs together, then both left legs, causing it to sway side to side. Sway with it, and you won't fall off.

HOW TO STOP A RUNAWAY CAMEL

1 Rein it in (sideways).

At speeds up to 40 miles per hour (64 kph), a runaway camel ride is no pony trot. You need to rein in your dashing dromedary. But don't pull back—that could snap the reins. Instead, pull the reins to one side. This will cause the camel to run in circles. Pull toward the side that the camel seems to prefer, not against it.

2 Hang on for your life.

Pretend you're in a rodeo, and while you may need to hang on for more than 8 seconds, it won't be *too* long. Get low, grip the camel with your legs, and hold onto the horn of the saddle tightly. The camel will eventually get tired of running in circles and realize it isn't really getting anywhere.

3 Make your perfect dismount.

The camel will sit when it gets tired, giving you a perfect chance to hop off. Tell the camel "good boy" for sitting. Give it a treat.

Spit Take

You may have heard that irritable camels will spit on people. Is it true? Yes and no. Camels rarely spit and are generally good-natured. However, if a camel feels threatened, it may spit at whatever is threatening it. Only, it's not really spit. It's worse. It's more like projectile vomit. A camel burps up the semi-digested food in its stomach into its mouth and then uses its lips to sling the goods. The result is a stream of stomach stuff that can cover your entire upper body!

CHAPTER 4

How to Survive in the Jungle

How to Cross Piranha-Infested Waters

What's worse than the worst day you've ever had at school? Spending a day in a school of piranhas. With their super-sharp teeth (which can bite through a steel fishhook!), a school of piranhas can strip the flesh from a fish or small animal in seconds. Here's how to stay off the menu.

1 Choose the non-piranha section of the restaurant, er, river.

The safest section of a river is away from the fishing docks. Docks where fish are cleaned are like fast-food restaurants for piranhas (complete with swim-through service and snappy meals).

FAST FACTS • Piranhas mostly live in South American rivers, like the rivers in the Amazon rain forest. People in the Amazon region have used piranhas' sharp teeth as tools.

② Flee the frenzy.

In a "feeding frenzy," piranhas will snap wildly at anything in reach. Even though you are unlikely to be the main course, don't let any parts of you become a side dish. Piranhas generally eat fish that are smaller than they are, so they'll only bite you if you get in the way.

③ Nighttime is the right time.

If you absolutely must cross a piranha-infested river, do it at night. The fish are less active, and if you awaken them, they're likely to swim away. Dawn is the worst time for a dip, as piranhas are hungriest in the morning.

What Would You Do?

You're bushwhacking in the Amazon in search of an ancient relic rumored to have mystical powers. You machete your way through the underbrush and come upon a river. The water is low since it's the height of the dry season. You're pretty scraped up from fighting through some thorns, and the water will feel good. Great time for a quick dip, right?

Answer: No chance. Crazy Pants. Piranhas can be dangerously hungry during the dry season, especially if they smell the blood from your wounds.

How to Escape the Grip of a Python

The world's largest snake, the python, can grow as long as a fire hose and as wide as a telephone pole. The reptilian giant is also a "constrictor," meaning it squeezes its catch in its coils until the pressure is too much to take. Here's how to avoid the Hug of Doom!

1 **Be on the lookout.**
Pythons are all about the ambush. If that branch is moving, get your patootie out of there. Pythons can strike suddenly. They can also stay underwater for 30 minutes.

2 **Remain still.**
If a python manages to give you a squeeze, relaxing your muscles may trick the snake into thinking you've been properly tenderized and are ready for consumption. He may loosen his grip. If so . . .

3 **Go for the head.**
Take off your reptilian body wrap. Just grab the head and unwrap it. Hey look, you shouldn't have tried it on in the first place.

What's Your Worst Case?

Sharing a sleeping bag with a python?

or

Taking a bath with a school of piranhas?

Who Would Win in a Fight— an Alligator or a Python?

In 2005, a 13-foot (4-m) python and a 6-foot (2-m) alligator were found in an unusual position. The lifeless alligator was discovered sticking out from a tear in the equally lifeless snake's body. The snake probably thought it had won the battle after it swallowed the gator. However, it's not over till it's over, and unfortunately, in the end, it was over for both of them.

How to Escape from Quicksand

How many times have you been walking to school when BAM!, you suddenly stumble into a pit of quicksand? OK, so maybe quicksand isn't as common in daily life as cartoons seem to indicate. But if you're walking around the right (or wrong) riverbank, you just may encounter that rare substance that's created when water mixes with sand but doesn't form clay. Which makes it extra sticky and possible to sink into—like a big bowl of earth pudding!

1 **Walk softly and carry a big stick.**

If you're in quicksand country, bring a pole. The pole will help you if you get stuck. Try not to step anywhere that looks suspicious, like onto a sand-topped puddle or in the hole by that sign that says "quicksand."

2 **If you start to sink, lay the pole on top of the quicksand.**

Think of the pole as one of those foam-noodle-floaty things at the pool. Moving slowly, wiggle your back onto the "noodle" and slowly spread your arms and legs. Chill out until you start to float.

BE AWARE • Always move slowly in quicksand. Thrashing around will tire you out and puts you at risk of inhaling sand, which can suffocate you.

3 **Float, don't flap.**

OK, so you forgot your pole. Don't panic: Your body is less dense than quicksand, so if you can relax, you will eventually begin to float. If you have a heavy backpack, shrug it off—anything that makes you heavy will make you sink.

How to Deal with an Angry Gorilla

There's a reason for the expression "to go ape"—a gorilla will scream, beat his chest, and bare his teeth when upset. Of course, it's all just a big show to look tough and assert the gorilla's rank in the group. To stay safe, you need to learn your role.

1 Let's get ready to humble!

Gorillas are usually pretty peaceful—unless you're threatening them. So swallow your pride and let the gorilla win the staring contest. Stay quiet and keep your arms to your side, so he doesn't think you're testing his dominance.

2 Don't call his bluff.

A gorilla may make a "bluff charge" to intimidate you. Well, be intimidated. If you're nose-to-nose with a 400-pound (181-kg) gorilla, make yourself small and act afraid. If he thinks you got his point, he'll let you off easy.

3 Offer groom service.

So you've just been charged by a giant ape. Caressing the mad monkey's fur probably seems like odd advice. In this case, however, the ape may take the hair care as a nonthreatening gesture, because lower-ranked gorillas will groom the head ape. In other words, if you can't beat 'em, groom 'em.

How to Remove a Leech

In the warm shallows of jungle pools lurks a little blood-sucker that loves to latch onto unsuspecting swimmers like you. Here's how to avoid being a leech's juice box.

1 Don't start in the middle.

When you find a leech stuck on you, resist the urge to just grab the leech in the middle and pull. The leech is lip-locked on your arm in not one, but two places! Playing tug-of-war with your own body is a game no one wins.

Leech Anatomy

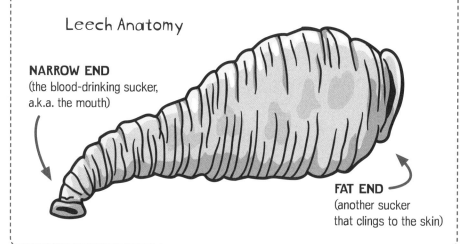

NARROW END
(the blood-drinking sucker, a.k.a. the mouth)

FAT END
(another sucker that clings to the skin)

2 Nail the leech.

Look for the small end of the leech—this is the mouth. Put your fingernail on your skin next to the leech, but not directly on it. Push against it sideways to break the seal.

3 So long, sucker!

Now push away the big end, while flicking at the mouth so it doesn't reattach. Fling the leech away, shaking it off your finger like an unwanted booger.

How to Catch Fish Without a Rod

Anybody can catch a fish with a motorboat, a fancy rod, and a state-of-the-art lure. The test of a true fishing master is whether you can catch a fish with nothing but the clothes on your back. Literally.

1 Make the frame for a net.

Find a young plant that splits into two branches, like the one shown on the right. It should be about as long as your leg. Bend the two branches toward each other and tie them together to make a circle.

2 Take the shirt off your back.

And your front. Don't forget your arms. In fact, take the shirt off completely! After you take off your shirt, tie a knot in the shirt below the armpits. Then tie the shirt to the sides of the net frame. Voilà, a net!

3 Stay out of the sun.

This is about catching fish, not rays. Fish like the shadowy places near the edges of the water, so that's your target area. Once you find the right spot, it's time to . . .

4 Net the surf.

When you swipe your homemade net through the pool, water should flow through the shirt, but fish will be caught.

How to Build a Shelter in the Rain Forest

With a name like "rain forest," it's probably going to rain in this forest—a lot. Which means that if you're lost here, you need to find (or make) some cover fast.

1 Location. Location. Location.

High and dry ground is ideal. Look for a clearing. Stay away from any swampy or low-lying spot, a.k.a. the mosquito breeding ground. And don't pick a spot under a coconut tree or a tree with any dead limbs, or else more than raindrops may fall on your head.

2 Lean on me.

Sticks and stones *can* protect your bones. Find a sturdy fallen tree trunk or a rock. Lean some thick branches and sticks at an angle against the fallen tree. This is why this sort of shelter is called a "lean-to." Crawl under it to make sure you have enough room to fit (your lean-to shouldn't be too-lean).

3 Seal it up.

Fill in all the holes with lots of large leaves and moss. Pile it on! You don't want any leaks. Hang a "Do Not Disturb" sign on the side of your shelter, so the jungle critters will leave you alone.

The Rain Forest by the Numbers

- The Amazon rain forest alone produces 20 percent of Earth's oxygen.
- More than 3,000 fruits are found in rain forests.
- Some experts believe we are losing 50,000 plant species a year from the destruction of the rain forest.

Other Shelters

The lean-to is just one easy shelter to make. There are loads of others to choose from depending on your circumstances.

The Dry Inn

If you have a poncho and rope, you can use it, instead of the leaves, as siding.

The Swamp Bunk

If you can't find a site away from the swamp, then you need to elevate your game with a covered, raised bed made from four trees and lots of brush.

The A-Frame

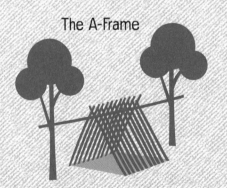

This is like a lean-to with two sides. Take a long log and balance it on a tree stump or rock. Then follow directions for a lean-to on both sides.

The Fantasy Fort

Who says rain forest living can't be posh? Just fly in an architect and some builders and make your abode a tad less humble. Star-gazing deck optional.

CHAPTER 5

How to Survive in the Arctic

How to Avoid a Polar Bear Attack

Here's the problem with polar bears: They have no natural predators, so they have little fear. This means they're not afraid of humans. All the more reason to watch your tushy on the tundra!

1 **If the bear doesn't see you, keep it that way.** Don't try to get a closer look or a better picture. Stay downwind of the bear, so it doesn't catch your funky odor. No offense.

2 **If the bear sees you, show you're only human.**
If you see the bear standing, sniffing, or taking notice of you, let the bear know you're human by talking and waving your arms. If you're in a group, everybody should do this. Make a commotion. Have a dance contest.

Real or Ridiculous?

a. Polar bears have clear hair, not white hair. The hair *looks* white because it reflects light.

b. Some polar bears in Antarctica have black hair.

c. Polar bears have webbed front feet.

d. Polar bears have been known to make snowman-like structures and rub their backs against them.

e. Under their fur, polar bears have spotted skin.

f. Polar bears have taste buds on their toes.

Answer: a and c are real. Choice b was doubly ridiculous— there *are* no polar bears in Antarctica.

3 Stand your ground.

If the bear charges, should you jump in the water? No good. Polar bears are great swimmers. Hit the ice? No dice. Polar bears are quite the speed skaters. And in the snow, forget about it. Your only chance is to pollute the atmosphere and increase global warming, thereby making these beasts extinct. Just kidding. If the bear *does* attack, you and the group all need to attack back. Hopefully the bear will retreat, giving you enough space to then leave the area.

How to Survive Falling Through the Ice

Let's say you're walking on ice. (Which you shouldn't do.) Then let's say you walk onto *very thin* ice. (Which clearly you shouldn't do. *Dude, what the heck is wrong with you?!*) It's too late now. You've fallen in—but the good news is, you *can* get out.

1 Inhale. Exhale. Repeat.

Guess what? The water is going to be cold. As in shockingly, gaspingly cold. Try not to hyperventilate; stay calm. Tread water.

2 Remember where you came from.

Chances are you just walked away from the strongest ice. So turn to face the direction you came from. Look for your foolish footprints or a landmark like a tree or building to locate your point of origin.

3 Elbows out.

Get your elbows on the ice and hoist yourself up but not completely out of the water. You just gained a few pounds

How to Rescue Someone Else Who Fell Through the Ice

If someone else breaks the ice, don't jump in, too. Instead of becoming a second ice cube, coach them out. If they can't do it, throw them a rope, hockey stick, or even a long branch. Just don't reach with your hands, or the panicked person might pull you in!

with your "liquid diet," so let the water weight drain from your clothes before trying to pull yourself up.

4 **Go kicking and screaming.**
Kick your feet as if you're swimming to propel yourself forward as you pull yourself up onto the ice.

5 **Roll on.**
When you get out, do not stand up. Instead, roll away. This spreads your weight out over the ice and makes you less likely to fall through for a second time. And since you've already been introduced to the frigid water, there's no need to break the ice again.

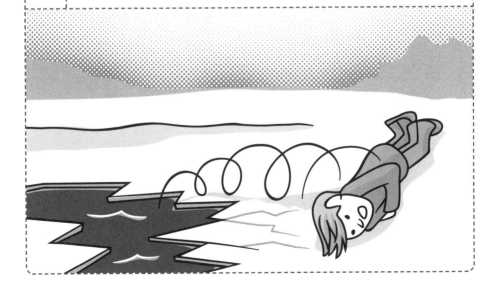

How to Deal with a Charging Moose

A moose is a lot like a Ferrari. It's shiny, sleek, and glamorous. OK, maybe not. But like a Ferrari, a moose can go from being completely still to moving very fast in a matter of seconds, bowling over anything in its way. Including you.

1 **Dog-gone it.**

To a moose, your dog looks a lot like a wolf. And a wolf is no friend to a moose. If you and Fido meet up with a moose, a) the dog is going to get upset and bark, b) the moose will think it has to defend itself, and c) the dog will then run back to its master. Which means, d) you are about to come face-to-face with an angry moose. So the moral of the story is: Don't bring your doggy on a hike in moose territory!

2 **Give it an escape route.**

Make sure the moose has a place to run other than over you. Generally a moose isn't looking to butt heads with you, and it will take a clear path if it has one.

Doodie Calls!

The Talkeetna Moose Dropping Festival is an annual celebration that has taken place in Talkeetna, Alaska, for more than 30 years. Varnished, numbered moose turds are dropped onto a target from a helicopter. People are given raffle numbers that correspond to the numbers on the turds. The closest turd to the target wins!

Moose Body Language

ears up

"Hm, what is that all about?"

hair up

"I don't like you. I think I'll knock you over."

"Would you like to join me for tea?" (rare)

③ Speak "Moose."

The moose may look at you with its ears up. If so, you can back away from the merely curious moose. If the moose lowers its head and the hair on the back of its neck stands up, then you need to start worrying.

④ Olé? No way!

If the moose charges, don't act like a matador. The bull of the north has a mighty set of antlers. Get behind something solid and stay as still as a pill until the moose has passed. In fact, stay put until the moose has left the area, resettled, and started a new life as an accountant.

How to Make Emergency Snowshoes

Why get exhausted and risk frostbite slogging through deep snow when you can make a pair of snowshoes and walk right on top of the snow surface? All you need is a pair of tree branches and a little string. Here's how to get your kicks on the snow.

1 Branch out.

You're shopping in Old Man Winter's shoe store, so the selection is limited. Look for two tree branches about 2 feet (.6 m) long. As far as style goes, you want branches with lots of little branches and green needles on them. It's all the rage on the tundra.

2 Step on it.

Time to try on your new shoes. Step on your gathered branches. About a hand's length of branch should stick out in front of your foot. The rest of the bushy part should be around and behind your foot.

3 Tie it up.

You'll need string. Good thing you brought some for that Arctic String Convention. If not, you might be able to use plant roots, or there may be a drawstring on your bag or coat that you can repurpose.

a) Tie one end of the string to the front of the branch.

b) Lace the string through the front holes of your shoe.

c) Tie the other end of the string securely to the branch.

4 Make them yours.

Carve or mark your new shoes with whatever symbols or stripes designate your favorite shoe brand.

Pick Your Kicks!

Which of the styles below is your best bet for snowshoeing?

The Fir Flop

The Pine Pump

The Beaver Boots

Answer: The Fir Flop. You want lots of little branches so your weight is spread out and you don't sink, like you could with a heel.

How to Build a Snow Cave

So you're camping out in the wintry wilderness, when a sudden gust of wind sends your tent off for a solo hang glide. You need a new shelter fast, or you'll soon be a snow angel. Here's how to stay warm and dry even when surrounded by snow and ice.

1 Find the right spot.

Look for a steep-ish slope with a buildup of snow that's soft enough to shovel but hard enough to pack together.

2 Dig it.

Every ice fortress needs a door. Dig an entrance tunnel straight into the slope about 3 feet (1 m) deep. Next, carve the main chamber in and upward from the end of the tunnel. Keep the chamber floor flat and make the ceiling domed. The entrance tunnel must be lower than the main chamber. Otherwise, snow could be blown or fall through the tunnel into the chamber.

3 Make it holy.

When finished with the main chamber, poke a ventilation hole though the roof. This will ensure you have enough air to breathe, and you'll be thanking yourself if your fellow snow-caver lets one rip in the night.

> **FAST FACT** • The Yupik Eskimos have more then 20 words for snow, including *muruaneq* (soft deep snow), *natquik* (drifting snow), and *kanevvluk* (fine snow particles). They do not have a word for snow that isn't deep enough to cancel school, though.

How to Survive If Stranded on an Iceberg

No matter how you got *on* this floating chunk of ice, here's how to make the best of it—and how to get off.

1 Build on your 'berg.

You need shelter. You can build a trench (a long hole covered by blocks of ice) or, if you see an extended stay in your future, build a snow cave (see page 99)— icebergs are almost always covered in snow.

2 Snow + sun = water.

The surface of an iceberg is made mostly of freshwater, so you can drink to your heart's desire. Put the snow or ice in a container and let the sun beat down on it. Eating snow is not the same as drinking water (eating uses your body's energy, sapping you of much-needed strength), so fully melt the snow first. As a last resort, scrape at the top ice to make your own personal snow cone. Flavor: plain.

3 Go fish.

In general, a human can go three days without water and three weeks without food. That's a theory you don't want to test. End your hunger strike as soon as you can. Make a fishing rod out of anything you can. If necessary, hunt sea birds with ice balls.

4 Catch my drift?

In Anarctica, icebergs drift clockwise around the South Pole. Keep your eye out for ships and weather stations. In the Arctic, the currents flow east to west. You may drift to populated areas near Greenland. Of course, this ride will take a few months, so you'll have time to decorate your mobile home.

Real or Ridiculous?

Nature is a master ice sculptor. Scientists classify icebergs with different names, depending on their shape. All the icebergs in the world are monitored so that another *Titanic* disaster can't occur!

Which of these iceberg shapes are works of nature and which are not?

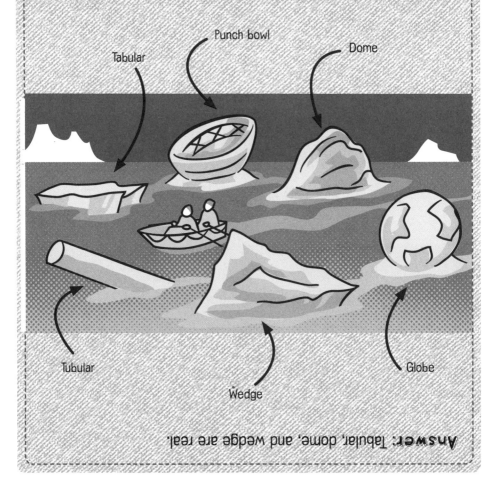

Punch bowl

Tabular

Dome

Tubular

Wedge

Globe

Answer: Tabular, dome, and wedge are real.

CHAPTER 6

How to Survive on Safari

How to Dress for Success on Safari

When a typical day on safari in East Africa may include meeting with lions, crocodiles, and elephants, looking fashionable may not be a top priority. But pick your clothing carefully: It's worth the effort to sport the right duds for your trip.

1 Be an onion.

This isn't about smelling bad or making people cry— this is about dressing in layers. You might be thinking, "It's gonna be steamin'!" Well, you're half right. It *will* be hot during the day. But night is a different story— believe it or not, it can get pretty cold in the African savannah.

2 Don't forget PJs.

In this case, PJs stand for "pull-over jackets." You'll want a warm jacket if you plan to be out or camp at night. Pack layers so you can control your temperature.

3 Hang loose.

Tight clothes are a bad idea. You'll often need to cover your whole body to protect against mosquito bites and sunburn, and loose clothes will keep you cooler in the heat. And cotton has a way of getting wet and staying wet, so wear fabrics that dry quickly next to your skin instead.

4 Accessorize.

Protect your head with a wide-brimmed hat, sunglasses, and some sunblock. Cover your feet in sturdy, comfortable walking shoes. Better yet, wear special hiking boots or lightweight, quick-drying shoes with thick soles.

5 Go khaki, not wacky.

Leave the Hawaiian shirt at home. Blending in with your environment is the goal, and khaki is ideal. Bright colors can alarm animals.

FAST FACT • The color blue can attract the tsetse fly, which carries a toxin that can cause the illness sleeping sickness, which causes fever, headaches, and joint pain, in addition to sleepiness.

Safari, So Good

Safari means "journey" in the African language of Swahili. Safaris used to be hunting trips, but these days, going on safari usually means traveling to a nature reserve in eastern or southern Africa, riding around in a car, and taking lots of pictures.

Safari-goers often search for the "Big Five" animals, but there are plenty of other great animals to see beyond these big shots. A short list is below, along with their Swahili names (which are pronounced just like they're spelled, for the most part).

Lion	simba
Elephant	tembo
Rhino	kifaru
Leopard	chui
	(pronounced "chewy")
Buffalo	nyati
Giraffe	twiga
Hippo	kiboko
Cheetah	duma
Zebra	punda milia
Gazelle	swara
Hyena	fisi

The Big Five { Lion, Elephant, Rhino, Leopard, Buffalo

How to Track Animals

Tracking is a crucial wilderness survival skill. Keep your eyes open for the signs an animal leaves, and you'll be able to avoid any predators and find the animals you *do* want to see when you're on safari.

1 Dust for prints.

Look for prints where impressions may be left, such as along streams or in dusty areas. Know the characteristic footprints of the critters you're interested in:

- Four toes per foot suggests dog or cat family.

- Elongated prints may be from the hoofs of a gazelle or giraffe.

- Comma-shaped prints might be a warthog or wild pig.

2 Be a poop-snooper.

Animals leave behind more than just footprints. Keep your eyes peeled for poop along the trail. The scoop on poop: If the animal is an herbivore (a vegetarian), it will leave round pellets. If the animal is a carnivore (meat-eater), its leavings will be long and tapered. It's your doodie, er, duty to track.

3 Watch their diets.

Knowing what comes out of an animal is important, but so is understanding what goes in. You gotta know what your animals like to munch on. Wildebeests eat the tops of grasses, while zebras mow their lawns down to the roots. Skilled trackers can even recognize the patterns of teeth marks on shrubs and bushes!

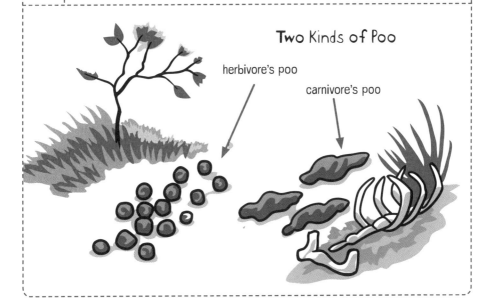

Two Kinds of Poo

herbivore's poo

carnivore's poo

How to Survive the Deadliest Animal in Africa

What do you think is the deadliest African animal? Go ahead, guess. The lion? The rhino? Wrong. The deadliest animal in Africa is no bigger than your fingernail. It's the mosquito. In Africa, mosquitoes can carry malaria, which kills up to two million people a year, so you want to be utterly repulsive to mosquitoes in Africa (or anywhere else where malaria is present). Here's how to get these pests to bug off.

1 Be as repulsive as possible.

Get an insect repellent with the chemical DEET. Spray it on your clothes and skin as directed.

> **FAST FACT** • Only female mosquitoes suck blood—they need it for their eggs. Both males and females eat flower nectar and other sweet-smelling foods.

2 Don't smell.

Avoid using hairspray, perfume, or other scented items that could smell sweet and attract the pests. If you smell like flowers or fruit, they'll think you're food.

3 Don't show skin.

At night, when mosquitoes are most active, cover your body from head to toe. Sleep in rooms with screened windows or under mosquito nets.

> **DID YOU KNOW?** • A small donation (as little as $10) can help a family in Africa get mosquito nets. If you want to help, just search online for organizations that take donations.

How to Escape from a Crocodile

How do you tell the difference between a crocodile and an alligator? Here's a rule of thumb: A crocodile has a long, narrow, V-shaped snout, while the alligator's snout is wide and U-shaped. Here's another rule of thumb: Never get close enough to be able to tell the difference.

1 Don't go it alone.

Never swim or boat by yourself in waters that are home to crocodiles. To a croc, a solo swimmer looks like a tasty treat, but a group of people just looks like trouble. Stay with your buddies.

2 Surrr-prise! *Not.*

If caught off-guard, a croc may attack on instinct. So if you suspect there could be one nearby, slap the water, shout, do impressions, sing your favorite song, whatever! Just make some noise.

3 Give it some space.

Crocodiles and alligators have been known to jump well out of the water to snag prey that thought it was safe to chill on low-hanging tree branches. If you see one, stay at least 20 feet (6 m) away from the water.

20 feet
(6 m)

4 | Do not feed the animals, please.

Feeding crocs can cause them to get over their fear of humans.

5 | Get out of the croc-pot.

Both crocs and gators have two sets of eyelids. They have a pair of clear inner lids that function as natural goggles and allow them to see perfectly underwater. Still think you're a match for Old Four-Eyes in the water? Consider this: Crocs have "skin sensors" that can sense vibrations when something enters the water. Bottom line: If you even suspect there's a crocodile around, get out of the water yesterday!

6 Run!

If you spot a croc on land, run. Run fast. Run straight. Run far.

3 Myths About Crocodiles and Gators

Myth #1: They're slow. A large croc can run 10 mph (16 kph), which is probably about the same speed you can run. Do the math. Actually you don't have time. Just run.

Myth #2: You should run in zigzags. This idea stems from the idea that crocs can only see straight ahead, so they'll lose sight of you if you zig and zag all over the place. However, you're better off running away any way you can. The more distance you can put between you and the croc, the better.

Myth #3: Crocs like to chase people. Actually, they're not like lions. They don't like to chase down their prey. They're way too cool for that. They're lurkers. They lie low before attacking.

How to Survive an Elephant Stampede

Sure, elephants may look big, clumsy, and slow, but they can actually run faster than 25 mph (40 kph). Their speed and strength makes elephants the linebackers of the Animal Kingdom. And while a herd of charging pachyderms can be scary, stay calm. Do the wrong thing, and you'll soon be elephant toe-cheese.

1 Take cover.

Running's not an option—the elephants will just catch up. Instead, find a sturdy structure to get into. Of course, there aren't always a whole lot of sturdy structures on the African plains. So . . .

2 Grab a trunk.

Of a tree, not an elephant! If you're a skilled tree-climber, you might be in luck. Elephants, even in a frenzied stampede, will try to avoid trees. Grab a branch and hoist yourself up, staying close to the trunk. If you can't climb a tree, huddle close to the tree trunk. *Be* the tree trunk.

③ Get down.

This might sound crazy, but if all else fails, lie down. Unless it sees you as a threat, an elephant is unlikely to step on you. If you stay standing, you run a higher risk of getting shish-kebab'ed on an elephant's tusk.

Do not grab an elephant trunk.

Being sneezed on **or** Falling in a pile of
by an elephant? fresh elephant poop?

How to Survive a Charging Rhinoceros

The black rhino has a horn on its face and a chip on his shoulder. If one lowers its horny head and snorts at you, it's got goring you on its mind. You don't want to be on the receiving end of the charge from an animal that weighs more than a ton. Here's how to avoid it entirely.

1 **Tree up, don't tee up.**
At 30 mph (48 kph), a charging rhino is not outrunnable. If one comes at you, climb a tree. Make sure you get higher than the horn can reach, or you're just teeing yourself up for the rhino.

2 **Scrub-a-dub-dub.**
If you can't get to a tree, the next best thing is thick, scrubby brush. Get as far into the bush as you can. Don't worry, your panic will keep you from feeling the pricks of those sharp thorns. Better a thorn than a horn.

3 Opposites don't always attract.

Once you have avoided the charge, run in the opposite direction the rhino is running. These big boys don't like to turn around, so once they get going in one direction they're unlikely to reverse course. It's not a bullfight; you just need to avoid that first charge.

Real or Ridiculous?

The jolly-looking hippopotamus is actually one of the most deadly animals in Africa. Hippos are known for being aggressive when humans enter their territory, and they get particularly riled up when their path to water is blocked, as they spend most of their time underwater (even though they're mammals). Can you tell which of these hippo activities are real and which are ridiculous?

a. Hungry, hungry hippos have been known to tear full-grown crocodiles in half.

b. Hippos eat rocks to help them sink in the water.

c. A hippo is capable of jumping 2 feet (60 cm) in the air.

d. A hippo might fall asleep right in the water—and stay underwater for as long as five minutes before surfacing to breathe, all without waking up.

e. Baby hippos are born underwater, then they swim to the surface for air.

f. Hippos spin their tails to spread their poo, to mark their territory.

Answer: a, d, e, and f are true.

Appendix

HOW TO TELL DIRECTION WITHOUT A COMPASS

The Stick Shadow Method

1. Stand a stick up in the ground.
2. Mark the tip of the shadow of the stick.
3. Mark it again 15 minutes later.
4. Draw an imaginary line from the first line to the second. The line points east.

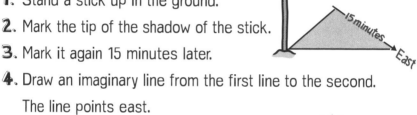

The Watch and Learn Method

1. Hold your watch so that the hour hand points directly at the sun.
2. Imagine a line halfway between the hour hand and the 12. That line will be pointing south.

OTHER WAYS TO TELL DIRECTION

- Most moss grows on the north side of trees.
- Spiderwebs are often built on the south side.
- Clouds often travel west to east.

Appendix

HOW TO SIGNAL FOR HELP

Third Time's the Charm

A series of three is the universal call for distress. If you have a whistle, blow it three times to call for help. If you have three pieces of bright material (a tent, poncho, tarp, etc.), set them side by side in a clearing so they can be seen by a plane flying by. Three rock piles will work as well.

Steer the Mirror

On sunny days, you can signal for help with a mirror or anything shiny that reflects light.

Appendix

FIELD GUIDE TO EXTREME FOODS

While on your travels, you are likely to encounter some pretty extreme foods. Know what they'll taste like before you take a bite with this handy chart.

Place	Food	What It Tastes Like
Ecuador	Guinea pig	Chicken
China	Turtle shell gelatin	Bitter cola
Tibet	Yak butter tea	Oily, salty tea with sour milk
Shanghai	Duck heads	Chewy chicken
Egypt	Camel	Grainy and fatty beef
Philippines	Sautéed crickets	Crunchy, buttery chewy morsels

Place	Food	What It Tastes Like
Hong Kong	Snake soup	Chicken broth with fish
Cambodia	Deep-fried spider	Crab with gooey black juice
Scandinavia	Lutefisk (air-dried whitefish prepared with lye)	Soapy, fishy gelatin
Morocco	Pigeon pie	Chicken pot pie
Mexico	Corn fungus	Mushrooms on the cob
France	Pâté (spreadable liver)	Wet cat food
Scotland	Haggis (sheep stomach lining stuffed with minced organ meats)	Wet cat food mixed with oatmeal, served in a balloon. (Do not eat the balloon.)
Your House	Fried chicken	Guinea pig, duck heads

Appendix

FOREIGN EMERGENCY PHRASES

Brazil (Portuguese)
Do those fish have teeth?
Aqueles peixes têm dentes?
a-KEH-les PEH-shehs teng DEHN-ch.

Kenya and other parts of Africa (Swahili)
Excuse me, there seems to be a large lion behind me.
Kubwa simba nyuma mimi.
CUB-wuh SIHM-buh NYOO-muh ME-ME.

Norway (Norwegian)
I'm sure that ice is safe to walk on.
Jeg er sikker på at den isen er trygg å gå på.
Yay ehr SEEK-er poh at dehn EE-sen ehr treeg oh goh poh.

Indonesia (Indonesian)
Look out! There's an orangutan behind that tree—maybe he wants your banana!
Awas! Ada orangutan* di belakang pohon itu—mungkin dia mau pisang kamu!
Ah-WAHS! Ah-dah ore-AHNG-oo-tahn dee beh-LAH-kahng poe-hone EE-too—MOONG-kin DEE-ah mao PEE-song KAH-moo!

* The Indonesian word *orangutan* means "person of the forest" (*orang* = person; *hutan* = forest).

About the Experts

These experts reviewed all the tips in this handbook and offered their extremely good advice. Consider them the coaches of Team Extreme!

"Mountain Mel" Deweese has more than 30 years of worldwide experience teaching survival skills. His work has spanned the globe, from the Arctic to the tropics, and he has dealt with animals of all sorts. He has shared wilderness survival skill knowledge with more than 100,000 students around the world and continues to do so through his Web site, www.youwillsurvive.com.

John Lindner is the director of the "Wilderness Survival School" for The Colorado Mountain Club, and he runs the "Snow Survival School" for Safety-One International, Inc. A former instructor for Denver Public Schools and the Community College of Denver, John has taught mountaineering and survival training for almost 30 years.

Charles Maciejewski has a degree in Adventure Education and has worked at Outward Bound, the Bronx Expeditionary Learning High School, and the Kurt Hahn Expeditionary Learning School. He has planned numerous urban and wilderness expeditions with students and trained teachers on doing work in nature. He loves the natural world, cycling, and snowboarding.

About the Authors

David Borgenicht is a writer, editor, publisher, and the coauthor of all the books in the Worst-Case Scenario Survival Handbook series. He has been known to float on quicksand, overpack while on safari, and employ "the standard squat" (see page 48). He lives in Philadelphia.

Justin Heimberg defines the word *extreme*. He is extremely cautious and wary. He is an extreme sleeper and an extreme television watcher. On the rare occasion when Justin is not being extreme, he writes books and films. He lives in an extreme suburb in Maryland.

About the Illustrator

Chuck Gonzales is a New York City–based illustrator who was raised in South Dakota. He's no stranger to worst cases, having illustrated *The Worst-Case Scenario Survival Handbook: Junior Edition*. Growing up in the Dakotas, he is very familiar with surviving on the tundra.

The
WORST-CASE SCENARIO
Survival Handbook:

WEIRD

Junior Edition

The
WORST-CASE SCENARIO
Survival Handbook:
WEIRD
Junior Edition

By David Borgenicht and Justin Heimberg
Illustrated by Chuck Gonzales

chronicle books · san francisco

A WORD OF WARNING: It's always important to keep safety in mind. If you're careless, even the tamest activities can result in injury. As such, all readers are urged to act with caution, ask for adult advice, obey all laws, and respect the rights of others when handling any Worst-Case Scenario.

Copyright © 2010 by Quirk Productions, Inc.

 A QUIRK PACKAGING BOOK.
All rights reserved.

Worst-Case Scenario® and The Worst-Case Scenario Survival Handbook™ are trademarks of Quirk Productions, Inc.

iPod, Velcro, and Super Soaker are registered trademarks of Apple Computer, Inc., Velcro Industries B.V., and Hasbro respectively.

Book design by Lynne Yeamans.
Typeset in Adobe Garamond, Blockhead, and Imperfect.
Illustrations by Chuck Gonzales.

Library of Congress Cataloging-in-Publication Data
Borgenicht, David.
  The worst-case scenario survival handbook : weird junior edition / by David Borgenicht and Justin Heimberg ; illustrated by Chuck Gonzales.
    p. cm.
  ISBN 978-0-8118-7438-0
  1. Curiosities and wonders—Juvenile literature. 2. Survival skills—Juvenile literature. I. Heimberg, Justin. II. Gonzales, Chuck. III. Title.
  AG243.B64 2010
  001.9—dc22
  2009039187

Manufactured by Toppan Leefung, Da Ling Shan Town, Dongguan, China, in June 2010.

10 9 8 7 6 5 4 3 2

This product conforms to CPSIA 2008.

Chronicle Books LLC
680 Second Street, San Francisco, California 94107

www.chroniclekids.com

CONTENTS

Welcome to Weird

Your life may already have some "weird" in it—that neighbor who dresses her dog in a fuzzy pink sweater, that kid at school who picks his nose with his thumb—but there's a whole other level of weird out there. (Cue eerie music.) Werewolves, dragons, Bigfoot, UFOs, zombies, ghosts: These are the norm in the world of the weird.

Navigating this weird world can be a dangerous proposition. One run-in with a giant could be your last. One encounter with a zombie, and you may become one, too. One sneak peek at Medusa, and you may never sneak again.

But fear not. This handy guide will prepare you for encounters with all sorts of monsters and mayhem and fantastic phenomena. You'll know just what to do if you

find yourself face-to-fanged-face with a hungry vampire. You'll learn how to survive if you crash-land on Mars. You'll discover how to make the most of a time-travel journey, how to get through the night in a haunted house, how to outwit a leprechaun, and much more. By the time you're done with this book, you'll know how to pull off a whole host of feats that put the "super" in supernatural.

And although many of these strange scenarios are the stuff of science fiction and fantasy, there *are* facts in this book. You'll find plenty of real science. (Did you know that

Mars has a volcano three times the size of Mount Everest?) You'll also delve into folklore, literature, and history. (Do you know what ancient Romans used instead of toilet paper? You will soon!)

In fact, sometimes, fact is stranger than fiction—like the fact that there is a real organization called the Search for Extraterrestrial Intelligence, or SETI Institute, currently scanning space for signs of alien life. Even weirder, a real-life unicorn exists in Italy. (Well, something pretty close to one, anyway.)

So grab a candle and tiptoe down the dark corridor of the strange and scary. Expect the unexpected. Imagine the unimaginable. Open your mind to the impossible. Things are about to get weird.

—*David Borgenicht and Justin Heimberg*

Aliens and Other
Outer-Space Oddities

How to Handle a UFO Sighting

It's a bird. It's a plane. It's a...wait—no, it isn't. What *is* it? You know that it's flying, and you know that it's some sort of object. Could it be...? Are you *really* witnessing an unidentified flying object, otherwise known as a UFO? Here's how to know.

1 Clock it.

Look at your watch or cell phone and note the exact time of your sighting. This step is super important because you'll want to see if other people reported seeing the same thing at the same time.

2 Observe and document.

If you have a device that takes pictures or video, start shooting. Otherwise, fetch a pen and paper. Spare no detail—write it *all* down and make a sketch of what you saw. Ask yourself:

• *What was the shape and color of the UFO?*

- *Was the object moving? Vertically, horizontally, or both? Was it landing or taking off?*
- *Did anything unusual happen during the sighting (electricity flickering on and off, animals acting strangely, etc.)?*
- *Any noise? What did it sound like?*
- *Am I nuts?*

BE AWARE • UFOs have turned out to be meteors, new military planes on test flights, weather balloons, and the work of pranksters playing with video cameras.

3 Report.

If you really think you've seen a UFO, work with an adult to report your sighting to local police and an agency that specializes in UFO sightings, like the National UFO Reporting Center in Davenport, Washington.

Interview with an Alien Hunter

Seth Shostak is a senior astronomer at SETI Institute (Search for Extraterrestrial Intelligence), an organization of scientists and educators who are scanning deep space for signs of life.

Q: What type of signals is SETI Institute listening for?
A: We listen for radio signals that are produced by a transmitter. Many things in the sky also make radio noise—the sun, for example. Strange objects like pulsars, quasars, and big black holes also produce natural radio static. But in our SETI experiments, we look for a signal that only a transmitter could make—a signal that's at only one spot on the radio dial. This signal would tell us there's someone out there who's intelligent enough to invent radio.

Q: Is there a specific area of space you're focusing on?
A: Most of the time, we point our antennas at nearby stars. We hope that at least some of the stars will have planets like Earth with intelligent life. Our antennas are very sensitive. They could pick up a transmitter with the power of a cell phone if it were on Jupiter. An extraterrestrial's broadcast could be found even if it comes from hundreds of trillions of miles away, which is the distance of the nearest stars.

Q: Have you pictured the extraterrestrials you're looking for?

A: In movies and on television, most aliens look like us—with two eyes, two arms, and two legs. There's no reason to think that real extraterrestrials would resemble Earthlings—after all, they've developed on an entirely different planet. It's possible that we might even detect aliens that aren't living but are some sort of thinking machines.

Q: Why is SETI Institute's research important?

A: Science is all about curiosity. We just want to know how the universe works. In a universe with ten thousand billion billion visible stars, could it be that this is the only world where intelligent life exists? Wouldn't you want to know if others are out there?

Q: If you ever have the chance to meet extraterrestrial life, what's the first thing you'd ask?

A: I would ask, "Do you have music?"

How to Survive an Alien Abduction

You're taking out the trash, minding your own business, when you're suddenly blinded by a bright light. Hovering above you is a flying saucer, and the aliens inside have their eyes on *you*. Before you can say "E.T., go home," you're being sucked into their spaceship! Here's how to handle those uninvited visitors from space when they try to get their tentacles on you.

1. Stay calm.

No need to freak (just yet). If the aliens think you're a threat, they might zap you with electric lances, phasers, or some alien technology that can toast an Earthling in nanoseconds. Be agreeable and remember that aliens probably don't have the same customs as you and your friends. If you reach out to shake their hands, the gesture may mean "Hello, I want to destroy you!" in Zorzootzese, so follow their lead when it comes to greetings. (Or just don't move at all.)

2. Show your chill skills.

It's possible that the aliens only want to check you out, boast about the size of their catch to their buddies back home, take a picture with you, and then let you go. Your best bet? Wait it out before breaking out your alien-busting moves and trying to make a Great Escape.

Being captured and put in a zoo for alien entertainment?   **or**   Being used as a lab rat for the advancement of alien science?

3 Get to know 'em.

It's not every day that you get to hang out with alien-kind. So, make it your mission to find out all the deets. Use pictures, pantomime, whatever it takes to communicate. Which galaxy are they from? What does their planet look like? What tunes do they have on their alien iPods?

4 Be a secret apprentice.

If it becomes clear that the aliens don't plan on throwing you back into Earth's pond, your only chance to get back home is to fly there yourself. But before you go conking two aliens' big-brained heads together to knock them out, study their piloting techniques and understand how to operate the UFO's navigation system. Otherwise, you'll be stranded in space. Forever.

What I Did on My Alien Vacation

People claiming to have been abducted by aliens often tell similar stories. Here's what you might expect from a flying-saucer escapade:

- **Capture.** You are removed from your earthly surroundings.

- **Examination.** Your body is scanned by a strange contraption.

- **Conference.** The aliens speak to you.

- **Tour.** You're given a guided tour of the spacecraft.

- **Journey.** You go for a joyride around the solar system.

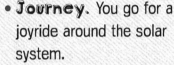

- **Return.** You are taken back to the place where you were captured, or sometimes to a different place.

How to Survive Landing on Mars

You're zipping by Mars for an up-close look at the Red Planet when—*wham!*—a rogue space rock slams into your ship. Your navigation functions are wiped out, but you still manage to touch down on the planet's surface. Now you just need to stay alive, Martian style.

1 Stay inside.

Because of its thin atmosphere, Mars offers little protection from radiation from space. Mars is also known for sandstorms that can cover the entire planet. Your best bet is to remain in your spaceship to stay protected from the elements. You don't want to end up as a sand sculpture. But if you *must* venture out…

2 Suit up.

Always wear your airtight space suit. The Martian atmosphere is 96 percent carbon dioxide, so your space suit will provide the oxygen you need to breathe.

③ Head to the poles.

If you run out of water, travel in your spaceship (assuming you're able to get your navigation functions up and running) to one of Mars's poles. Water has been discovered there (in the form of ice), and you won't have to dig very deep to reach it. You'll need to bring the Mars-cicles back to your ship to melt, unless you're in the mood for a Martian snow cone.

4 Consider the caves.

So you're out and about, taking in the Mars scenery, when sand starts swirling around. Before you know it, you're caught in the middle of a massive sandstorm! If your ship isn't close by, duck into a cave for extra protection. If you happen to be near Olympus Mons, you'll find seven caves (known as the "Seven Sisters") nearby. Just remember to stay in that suit!

5 Grow your own oxygen.

Running low on oxygen during your extended stay on Mars? Make oxygen from the Red Planet's dirt. In 1976, NASA's *Viking* lander poured water on Martian soil to see if plants would grow, and oxygen gas sprung up instead. Chemicals in the dirt called peroxides break down and release oxygen when they come into contact with good ol' H_2O. So, bring some Martian dirt into your spacecraft and see if you can refill your supply!

No Crash Zones

In case of spaceship malfunction, avoid landing on these planets...

- **Neptune.** This is the windiest place in the solar system, so your spacecraft would not fare well here!

- **Saturn.** Its rings might be cool to look at, but landing on this planet is far from pretty. Don't expect to land on any surface—there isn't one.

- **Mercury.** The planet nearest to the sun, Mercury has daytime temps as high as 840 degrees Fahrenheit (450 degrees Celsius), and lows of −275 degrees Fahrenheit (−170 degrees Celsius).

- **Jupiter.** This multicolored gobstopper of a planet is so big, you could stuff more than 1,000 Earths inside it. But that doesn't mean you can land here. This giant is full of so much gas, you'd eventually be crushed by the high pressure if you entered its atmosphere.

How to Deal with a Long Space Voyage

Congrats! You're back from Mars and ready for your next mission—this time you're going way out, beyond the solar system in search of new planets! This is the journey of a lifetime. Here's how to sit back, relax, and enjoy your extra-long flight.

① Fuel up...

But don't bother with bread—the crumbs will float all over your ship. Make a PB&J sandwich with tortillas instead. And rather than sprinkling on salt and pepper, *inject* your food with saltwater and pepper *oil*. Don't forget the hot sauce—a favorite of NASA astronauts—because your sense of taste gets weaker in space.

FAST FACT • To conserve water, astronauts don't rinse and spit after brushing their teeth. That means you'll have to rinse and *swallow* with special astronaut toothpaste.

② Work out.

Being weightless in space means your muscles don't have to work hard to hold you up against gravity. You can lose muscle and bone strength on your long voyage. To avoid pain when you step back on Earth, exercise on a space treadmill. Large elastic bands will hold you down as you run so you won't fly off.

BE AWARE • Cuts don't heal quickly in space, so be extra careful when handling sharp objects.

3. Dress for success.

You can wear comfy pants and socks in your ship, but venturing *outside* requires top-to-bottom protection. Your space suit will keep you alive during your space walk, which can last more than six hours. Your suit will give you oxygen, protect you from space radiation, and even give you water to drink. Some space suits even include a diaper known as a maximum absorbency garment—you'll need it if you're out for six hours!

4. Make a space playlist.

Before you take off, make sure to leave a playlist with Mission Control. The crew in Houston, Texas, will pipe your favorite tunes right into your ship to wake you up. Let's just hope your co-pilot's snoring doesn't drown out the music.

> **FAST FACT** • How do astronauts keep things from floating away in space? Velcro! Put Velcro on surfaces and even wear Velcro strips on your pants. Then place Velcro strips on objects, like books, clipboards, and meal trays, so you can pin them down securely—and use them!

Your Space Suit: Don't Leave the Ship Without It

Don't mess with outer space—it's hostile with a capital H. Here's what would happen if you didn't suit up before stepping out.

- **In space, there's no air,** and that means no air pressure to keep air contained in your lungs. So, it would all come rushing out in a big whoosh. That's called "taking your breath away." Big time.

- **The lack of air pressure** would also cause crazy things to happen to your blood and body fluids. They'd boil then freeze! Your boiling fluids would cause your internal organs and your skin to expand.

- **Micrometeoroids** (small particles of rock and dust) could slam into your body at high speeds. You could be hit by orbiting space trash, too.

How to Avoid a Black Hole

A black hole is born when a giant star collapses onto itself, creating a massive amount of gravity. A black hole's gravity is so strong that nothing—including light—can escape its pull. If light can't escape, neither can you. Here's how to avoid getting sucked in on your next intergalactic tour.

1 X-rays mark the spot.

Black holes are invisible because they're, well, black holes in space. But you can detect them by looking for their effects. If a black hole is close enough to a star, some of the star's gas can get pulled into it. As this gas plunges into the black hole, it gets very hot and gives off lots of energy in the form of X-ray light. You can use a special X-ray telescope to detect this radiation, like NASA's Chandra X-ray Observatory.

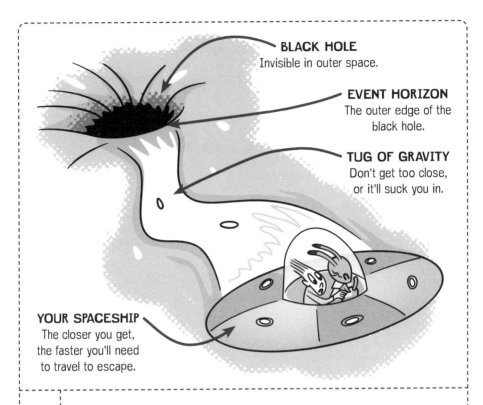

BLACK HOLE
Invisible in outer space.

EVENT HORIZON
The outer edge of the
black hole.

TUG OF GRAVITY
Don't get too close,
or it'll suck you in.

YOUR SPACESHIP
The closer you get,
the faster you'll need
to travel to escape.

2 Speed up!

If a black hole is all by itself out there in space with
nothing nearby to fall into it, your X-ray vision won't
help you. You won't notice the black hole until you
get close enough to feel a tug from its gravity. If this
happens, act fast! Really fast. The closer you get to a
black hole, the faster you'll need to travel to escape its
pull. How fast should you go? The fastest that anything
can go in the universe. That's the speed of light, which

is 186,000 miles (300,000 km) per second. At that speed, you'd travel around Earth eight times in a second. So, good luck with that.

3 Avoid the event horizon.

Let's say you didn't notice that your ship was heading toward a mysteriously dark spot in space. Unfortunately for you, if you get too close to a black hole, there will be nothing you can do to escape (not even traveling at the speed of light!). The "point of no return" is called the *event horizon*. If you cross it…

4 Prepare to be spaghettified.

Now it's time for the ultimate gravity experience: *spaghettification*. This term was coined by the physicist Stephen Hawking to explain the way gravity works when something falls into a black hole. Imagine your body being pulled in opposite directions while it's being squeezed very tightly. Okay, maybe you don't want to imagine that. A split second after you're spaghettified, you disappear into the hole, where all of your atoms get mushed into a single point (i.e., no more you). And you definitely don't want to imagine that!

CHAPTER 2

Monsters, Mummies, and More

How to Survive a Vampire Attack

Most modern-day vampires don't dwell in castles, don black capes, or announce in a Transylvanian accent, "I vant to suck your blood!" Today's vamp is a cool and cunning creature—suave, sophisticated, and expert at blending in with you and your friends. Don't be so bewitched (um, bevamped) that you forget what they're *really* after! Here's how to deal if a bloodsucker comes your way…

1 Look for (un)dead giveaways.
Vampires don't have a "vamp stamp," and they almost never wear a T-shirt that says, "I'm itching to sink my teeth into your neck." The good news is that there *are* clues you can count on. If you know what to look for, you'll be able to tell the true vampires from the wannabes and goth kids in no time.

How to I.D. a Vamp

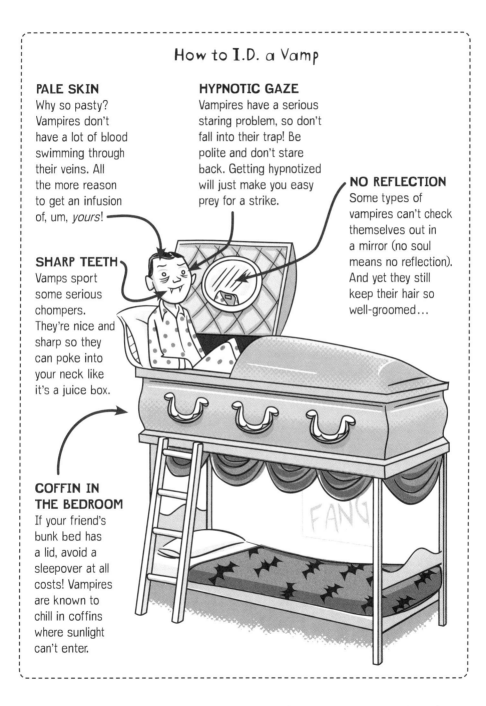

PALE SKIN
Why so pasty?
Vampires don't
have a lot of blood
swimming through
their veins. All
the more reason
to get an infusion
of, um, *yours*!

HYPNOTIC GAZE
Vampires have a serious
staring problem, so don't
fall into their trap! Be
polite and don't stare
back. Getting hypnotized
will just make you easy
prey for a strike.

NO REFLECTION
Some types of
vampires can't check
themselves out in
a mirror (no soul
means no reflection).
And yet they still
keep their hair so
well-groomed...

SHARP TEETH
Vamps sport
some serious
chompers.
They're nice and
sharp so they
can poke into
your neck like
it's a juice box.

**COFFIN IN
THE BEDROOM**
If your friend's
bunk bed has
a lid, avoid a
sleepover at all
costs! Vampires
are known to
chill in coffins
where sunlight
can't enter.

2 Secure your secret weapons.

Try these tricks to keep vamps at bay…

- **Garlic power.** Due to its strong smell and healing properties, garlic has been used across cultures for centuries as a defense against illness and evil spirits, including vampires. Always keep a couple of cloves in your pocket or backpack for emergencies. When you see a vamp, chew a clove and breathe in his direction.

- **Sunlight.** Vamps loathe the sun! If a vamp is hot on your heels, walk on the sunny side of the street. If you have a *serious* vampire problem, convince your family to make a permanent move to Yuma, Arizona, or Perth, Australia, two cities with over 300 sun-drenched days a year.

The Real Deal

There is such a thing as vampire bats. They feed on blood—the blood of rodents and small birds, that is! Native to Central and South America, these bats have heat receptors on their noses that help detect the spots where blood flows closest to their prey's skin.

What to Do if a Vampire Has a Crush on You

If this happens...	Do this...
That really pale, cute new girl in homeroom keeps staring at you...hungrily.	Offer her a slice of garlic-studded pizza. If she gets even paler, run.
Your best friend's cousin from out-of-town appears outside your window after dinner—and your room's on the second floor!	Hook up your sprinkler to some holy water and aim high.
A goth kid, who is new in town, suggests the two of you take a field trip to a dark cave populated with bats.	Suggest a trip to the beach instead. If he shows up completely covered in long pants and a hat the size of Texas, be wary. Also, if he wears socks and sandals, stay away! (He's not a vampire—he just needs a fashion revamp!)

From the Vault: Dracula

The world's most famous vampire is Count Dracula, who first appeared in Bram Stoker's 1897 novel, *Dracula*. Dracula was one of the first vampires in literature to be portrayed as intelligent and well-mannered. Until then, vampires were thought of as beastly. Some people believe that Dracula was actually based on a real-life Romanian prince named Vlad the Impaler. While Vlad wasn't really a vampire, having a nickname like that gives you a sense of the kind of guy he was!

- **Be cross.** Vampires cower at the sight of a cross, so sport a necklace with a cross pendant. If jewelry's not your thing, make a cross with rolled-up sheets of paper, drumsticks, lollipops…or just "cross" your fingers and hope for the best.

- **Soak 'em.** Consider visiting your local cathedral for a vial of holy water, which vampires can't stand. If a vampire comes looking for a "drink," douse him with a spray bottle, or fill up a Super Soaker and let it rip. Then make a run for it!

3 Fight for your life.

Vampires have superhuman strength and speed, so don't waste time trying out your kung-fu moves. Stake 'em instead. The best way to stop a vampire is the classic wooden-stake-through-the-heart method. You can whittle a spear out of a stick, a fence post, a chopstick, or even a croquet peg. Be creative!

How to Win a Zombie Showdown

Gaping wounds, decaying flesh, rotten stench...what's not to love about zombies? A zombie is a corpse that has been brought back to life through sorcery, a medical experiment, or a virus. These mindless maniacs survive on a steady diet of brains. So, before a pack of zombies can chow down on your cranium, use it to outwit the hungry horde.

1 Be dead-on with your zombie detection.
Your classmates might appear like zombies during class—think blank stares, groaning, bad posture—but there are a few telltale signs that they're not just spacing out. They might have caught the zombie bug!
- *When they wear purple, it brings out the dark circles under their eyes.*
- *They show up to science class only when animals are being dissected.*
- *They've developed a taste for the "tattered clothing" fad.*

- *They have really, really bad B.O.*
- *When they watch TV with you, instead of reaching for the popcorn, they reach for your pet frog.*

2 Distract one, distract them all.

Zombies are like sheep—they move in groups and tend to mindlessly follow the leader. If you can create a diversion to get one off your scent, like casually mentioning there's a sale on cerebellums at the mall, then there's a good chance you can escape from the pack.

❸ Don't get cornered.

Zombies are creatures of habit and hang out where they did when they were alive: the library, the classroom, the food court at the mall…. If you come across one, don't panic. Zombies are notoriously slow. Just avoid being the kid who is backed into a dead end or alleyway—like in every horror film ever made—and you should be fine.

> **BE AWARE** • A zombie's condition is contagious, so if one sinks its teeth into you, you'll be the newest member of the walking-dead club.

❹ Get a head.

If you find yourself surrounded by zombies and escaping isn't an option, you'll have no choice but to defend yourself. Like the mystery meat at your school cafeteria, almost nothing can destroy them…except for a well-placed blow to the head. So, keep *your* head when aiming.

How to Act Like a Zombie

Zombies are not the brightest bunch, so if you think you can't beat them, try joining them. It may be the only way to keep your wits.

Mumble, "Brains. Must get brains."

Read a zombie instruction manual.

Keep hair unkempt.

Grunt and groan.

Wear shredded, dirty clothes.

Stumble forward on right foot.

Slowly drag left foot behind you.

How to Make the Most of a Bigfoot Sighting

Rumored to be nearly 7 feet (3 meters) tall and 500 pounds (230 kg) of muscle and matted hair, Bigfoot has managed to stay hidden in the forests of North America for decades. Though many have claimed to have glimpsed him, the giant hairball just doesn't take a good picture. With these tips, you just might spot the elusive beast— *and* get the evidence you need to prove it.

1 **Go northwest.**

There have been over 500 sightings of Bigfoot in the wilderness of the Pacific Northwest, alone. (Plan your next trip accordingly.)

Your Bigfoot Checklist

- **Camera.** Carry one that doesn't have a delay in shooting time. He's big, but he moves fast...
- **Binoculars.** A quality pair will help you distinguish shapes and shadows in the trees.
- **Flashlight or night-vision goggles.** A must-have because Biggie's a fan of the nightlife.
- **Plaster of paris.** For when you come across his footprint and want to make a keepsake.

What (or Who) Is Bigfoot?

There are as many theories about Bigfoot (also known as Sasquatch) as there are hairs on his body. Some zoologists say he may be an unknown type of ape, while some Bigfoot believers think he may be from another planet. One of the most interesting theories is that Bigfoot is the "missing link," representing the stage of evolution between ape and man.

② Use common senses.

Obviously, you're looking out for the big-footed fella, but you also need to *listen* for him. Some Bigfoot observers claim that he makes sounds ranging from loud grunts to mournful cries. Keep your nostrils open, too. Reports note that Bigfoot has a strong, unpleasant odor. Imagine a cross between wet hair and spoiled salmon.

③ Be a track star.

Survival experts have perfected the art of "tracking," using footprints, droppings, and other signs to locate animals in the wilderness. Bigfoot (not surprisingly) leaves gargantuan footprints, and they could be your ticket to a sighting. It's good to go tracking right after it rains or snows when footprints are most visible.

④ Be quiet...until it's time to scream!

Bigfoot clearly doesn't like the limelight, so you'll need to be very quiet during your search. However, if you run into another big furry creature—like a mountain lion—you'll need to make as much noise as possible to prevent it from attacking.

The Bigfoot of the Lake

The Loch Ness Monster is an aquatic-looking dinosaur with a long neck, small head, bulky body, and long flippers. It is thought to dwell in the Scottish Highlands's Loch Ness ("loch" is Scottish for lake). If you think you've spotted Nessie, be aware of these illusions!

Volcanic gas

Rocks

Boat wakes

Logs

Synchronized swimmers

Hoaxes

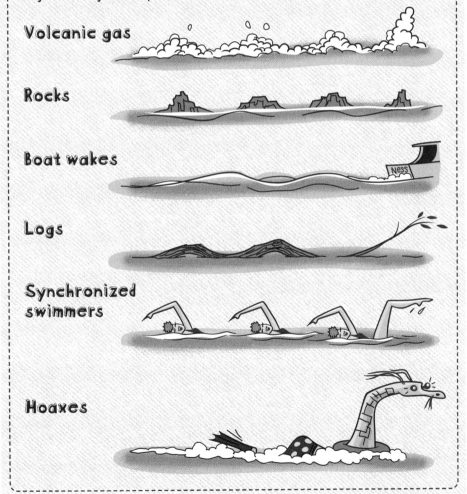

How to Manage a Mummy Encounter

You've been digging through the sands of the Sahara for months. Finally, you've found what you've been looking for: the entrance to an ancient tomb. Torch in hand, you creep inside. What might you find? And how will you avoid curses, booby traps, and...mummies? Read on.

1 Don't be a tomb raider.

An underground tomb is full of more than just a body. Mummies were often buried with all their belongings, including food, favorite pets, and even treasure! But consider this before taking any souvenirs: According to Egyptian legend, if you take anything from a tomb, you'll be cursed.

2 Let sleeping mummies lie.

The ancient Egyptians believed that bodies needed to be properly preserved with chemicals—and wrapped in bandages to keep them airtight—to ensure a safe passage into the afterlife. Since mummies are so serious about their eternal beauty sleep, they might be a tad crabby if disturbed. Oh, and some legends say a curse will befall anyone who bothers a mummy. Curses!

③ Booby traps? Ha.

Movies about mummies will make you think that tombs are full of booby traps. But really, no tomb has ever been found to have anything but a big slab of rock at its entrance. So, that's one thing you don't have to worry about.

How to Survive "Common" Tomb Traps

Although archaeologists have yet to find any traps in tombs, movies are full of 'em. Here's how you'd escape, Indiana Jones—style, if you were caught in a booby-trap scene.

- **The Hour Glass.**
  This trap causes sand to fill up a room. Cover your mouth with a bandanna or your shirt and put on shades to protect your eyes. Then clog the holes that the sand is pouring through with rocks or large gems. Act fast! You don't want to become the mummy's permanent roommate.

- **The Crusher.**
  This trap makes two walls close in on you. Look for a long statue, turn it on its side, and use it to brace the walls. Even if the statue doesn't hold, you'll at least have some time to get out and avoid getting squished into human hieroglyphs.

- **Flying Darts.**
  In this trap, you step on a loose stone and—*whoosh*—darts come flying at you. You'll be a goner if you set off this one, so step carefully to avoid becoming a pincushion.

4 Start a wrap battle.

Let's say the utterly ridiculous, totally unthinkable happens and a mummy awakens while you tiptoe through the tomb. When it comes charging after you, grab one of its loose bandages and start unraveling it, spinning the mummy like a top. When it gets too dizzy to chase you, wink and say, "It's about time you wound down."

The Writing on the Wall

Ancient Egyptian writing uses thousands of characters called hieroglyphs. Each hieroglyph represents a sound, a word, an object, or an idea. Hieroglyphs can be written left to right, right to left, or in columns.

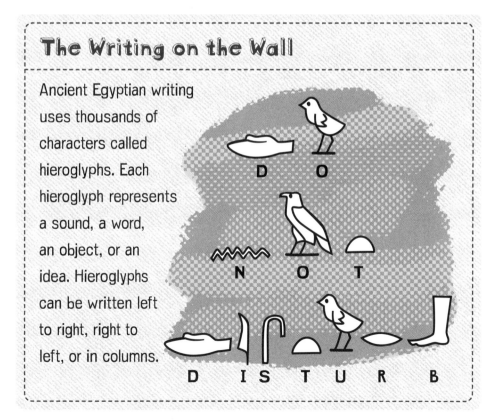

How to Survive a Werewolf Run-In

You're camping one night and decide to go for a stroll, when the misty clouds part to reveal a stunning full moon. Suddenly, you hear a chilling howl. A howl that can only mean one thing. Werewolf! *There* wolf. Harmless person by day, vicious wolflike beast by night, a werewolf is larger and stronger than your run-of-the-mill wolf (or human). Here's how to avoid the hairy, lunar beast.

1 ## Moon-watch.

Werewolves transform only during a full moon, so keep track of the lunar cycle to know when to be extra "were-y" and to keep your guard up. Once transformed, werewolves can't control their animal instincts. Luckily, a full moon occurs only once every 29 or 30 days, so you'll know exactly when to stay indoors.

2 ## Signs, signs, everywhere signs!

As the full moon approaches, watch for unusual behavior. Is your friend scratching behind her ear with her foot? Is your sister's hair looking especially thick and lustrous?

Werewolf Words

- **Lycanthrope.** (LIE-can-thrope) A fancy name for "werewolf" that comes from the Greek for "wolf man."

- **Transmogrification.** The sometimes painful process when a person changes into a werewolf. It's like instant puberty.

- **Wolfsbane.** A poisonous purple-flowered plant that wards off werewolves. Hooray for flower power!

Does your uncle get a five o'clock shadow (and an eight o'clock shadow…and a ten o'clock shadow)? Be*were* of potential transformations.

③ No biting!

Unless you have a desire to become part of the wolf pack, don't let Fido sink his fangs into you. Werewolf bites (and scratches) are infectious.

> **BE AWARE** • According to legend, if you drink water from a werewolf's footprint, you will soon become wolfkind. So, if drinking muddy water out of strange footprints is your thing, it might be time to switch to bottled water.

④ Go for the silver!

Gold is great for the Olympics, but when it comes to defeating werewolves, silver is number one (as in silver bullets, arrow tips, or swords). Aim carefully because you may only get one chance to stop a lunging werewolf. And what's worse than a lunging werewolf? A furious lunging werewolf.

CHAPTER 3

Hauntings and Other Mysteries

How to Navigate a Haunted House

Uh-oh. Your parents are going out of town and you're sleeping over at your great aunt's spooky, old house. It's not just the bugs, the odd smell, and the fluffy black mold that bother you—it's also that dreadful singing in the shower (when no one is in there!). Face it. The house is haunted. Here's how to stay comfortable in your own skin when it wants to crawl.

1 Don't go batty.

Haunted houses are like baseball dugouts. They're dirty, smelly, and full of bats. Bats can be frightening with their fast-flapping wings, screeching calls, and nocturnal schedule, but attacking humans is not their thing. Though they are almost blind, they use echolocation (sound waves to locate objects in their way), so they shouldn't fly into you.

❷ Skip the stairs.

Staircases are common haunted-house hazards. They can swivel, squeak, or even downright collapse. You don't want to head upstairs only to find out later that there's no way to get back down. If you can stay grounded on the ground floor at all times, you'll be better off. And, hey, ground floor means closer to the door!

Steer clear of cobwebs. Some spiders are venomous.

You may feel like you're being watched.

Bats are haunted-house fixtures.

Unsteady staircase may collapse at any moment. Stay on the ground foor.

Bring a lantern or flashlight to help light your way through the horrors.

World Famous Haunted Places

- **Tower of London, London, England.** The spirit of Ann Boleyn (King Henry VIII's second wife, who was beheaded in the tower in 1536) and troops of ghostly soldiers are thought to haunt this historic site.

- **The White House, Washington, D.C.** Spend the night in one of the haunted bedrooms, and legend says you just  might get a glimpse of the ghosts of Presidents Andrew Jackson and Abe Lincoln and First Lady Abigail Adams.

- **Catacombs, Paris, France.** The bones of more than six million Parisians are stored here, so you may want to skip this underground tour.

3 **Use some common spidey sense.**
Unlike bats, some spiders—like the black widow and black house spiders—are venomous. Also, where there are spiders, there could be cobwebs. Nothing is more spooky than walking through a web and then having to rip the sticky threads off your face. To avoid webs and spider bites, steer clear of dark nooks and crannies, especially in basements (this shouldn't be too hard!).

4 **Pull an all-nighter.**
Reality check: Do you really think you're going to get a good night's sleep in a haunted house? So, to calm your nerves, why not invite a friend or two over for a slumber party? You can have a pillow fight, play games, watch movies, and tell ghost stories…well, maybe not ghost stories.

5 **Study ghosts.**
The key to dealing with ghostly ghouls is to keep your fear in check, and the best way to do this is to arm yourself with knowledge. Turn the page to learn how to make the most of your ghost hosts.

How to Evict a Ghost

Bats, spiders, and sketchy staircases are one thing (or, uh…three things), but a ghost is what makes a haunted house truly haunted. Ghosts can be terrifying, angry, or just downright cranky. Here's how to get rid of an unwanted tenant, no matter what its temperament.

1 Politely ask the ghost to leave.

Yep, getting rid of a ghost can be that simple. Use a clear, firm voice but don't sound angry. If you explain why the

DO

DON'T

ghost is bothering you, it may respond to your logic and move on. No one wants to be a pest. Not even the dead.

Explain the whole "you're dead" thing.

A ghost doesn't always know it's dead, so it may carry on, making an omelet, not seeing that the eggs are going right through its hands. Do the ghost a favor and calmly explain, "You're dead." That way, it can move from the physical world to the spiritual realm (and leave you alone).

Be a problem solver.

Sometimes a ghost is sticking around because it wants to take care of some unfinished business, like giving a message to a loved one or searching for an important personal belonging. Consider helping the ghost so it can move on and out of your home.

BE AWARE • You may have a ghost buster in your very own garden! Paranormal researchers believe that if you burn sage and let the scent fill your home, a ghost will get the message to get out.

Your Neighborhood Ghost Guide

- **Phantom.** A ghost that resembles the living...until it walks through your wall.

- **Apparition.** A transparent ghost that appears like a fog.

- **Poltergeist.** An invisible ghost that makes a racket and moves things around without asking. Like the ghost version of a little brother!

- **Eau de toilette ghost.** A ghost with a strong scent of perfume or cologne.

4 Decorate your door.

According to Irish folklore, spirits won't enter a home if the door has been painted red. In Colonial America, people hammered decorative patterns of nails on their doors that were believed to guard against ghosts. Also, since ancient times, hazelnuts have been strung across doors to keep ghosts at bay. So, it seems like a good idea to do *something* with your door.

5 Live in harmony.

If all else fails and your ghost is of the extra-friendly variety, it might just be time to accept your ghostly fate—and your new roommate!

Shoe Ghost, Don't Bother Me!

According to folklore, if you place one shoe at the foot of your bed, facing one direction, and the other shoe facing the opposite direction, your home will be cleansed of ghosts. Of course, it might just be the nasty stench of your sneakers that gets rid of them!

How to Enhance Your ESP Powers

Ever just get a hunch about something? Maybe you sense what flavor you're about to pull out of a box of jelly beans, or which hideous cat sweater your teacher is going to wear today. If so, you just might have ESP or *extrasensory perception*—the act of receiving information without using any of the five senses, like sight or hearing. Even if forecasting the future doesn't come naturally, ESP is something you may be able to develop. Read on, and you may soon be reading people's minds.

1 Assess your skills.

Have you experienced these different types of ESP? If not, check out these tips.

- **Telepathy** is mind-to-mind communication. Ask a friend to think of a shape or object. Close your eyes and allow the image to form in your mind. Is it an apple? Or that weird foot-measuring device at the shoe store?

- **Psychometry** is the ability to learn the history of an object by touching it. Pick up something, like a used handkerchief. If you have this skill, visions of the handkerchief's life will play in your mind like a rapid-fire movie montage, including images of those who have blown their noses in it.

BE AWARE • Déjà vu is the mysterious sensation you get when you feel like you've witnessed or experienced something before.

- **Precognition** is the ability to view events before they occur. Look at your teacher and let your eyes unfocus. If you have this ability, a vision of the future should emerge, like that pop quiz you're not ready for. Be sure to distinguish between what is going to happen versus what you *want* to happen.

Work your muscles *and* your mind.

With ESP, you want to *feel* the answer. It's not like math where thinking out the problem helps. The more you think, the more you'll just cloud your "sixth sense." Some ESP experts say that you literally *feel* the knowledge in your body, meaning your muscles tense up when sensing signals.

Pick a card. Any card.

One way to enhance your mind-reading powers is to practice with playing cards. Can you predict the card you've chosen? Turn it over to find out.

> **BE AWARE** • Déjà vu is the mysterious sensation you get when you feel like you've witnessed or experienced something before.

4 Use your powers wisely.

Minds are like lockers. You really shouldn't go poking around in one that isn't yours. The exceptions are matters of life and death, like reading the minds of super villains who are up to no good, or figuring out if your crush likes you back…you know, matters of life and death.

Other ESP Powers You May Want to Try

- **Ocuphonics.** Knowing what the person on the other end of the phone looks like just by hearing his or her voice.

- **Photosmilia.** The ability to tell if someone is faking a smile in a photo.

- **Shakeosight.** The ability to know what's in a gift-wrapped present, just by shaking it.

How to Control Your Dreams

You're playing a game of kickball when, all of a sudden, your piano teacher winds up and rolls you a cantaloupe. And why are you dressed like a clown? You're dreaming! Sometimes it feels like you have no control over your dreams, but it doesn't have to be that way. You can learn to "awaken" in your dreams, get control, and do all kinds of cool stuff. Here's how.

1 Get plenty of sleep.

When you're asleep, your brain is most active during REM, or the Rapid Eye Movement stage. This stage is when most dreaming occurs. So, make sure you get at least eight hours of sleep to maximize your dreaming time.

2 Keep a dream journal.

If you want to learn how to control your dreams, you first need to remember them. The best way to improve your dream recall is to keep a "dream journal" by your bed. Any time you wake up during a dream, immediately write down what happened. Include every detail, no matter how bizarre.

③ Plan ahead.

Your dream journal is on your nightstand, and you're hitting the sack nice and early. As you go to bed, tell yourself you are going to realize you are dreaming. Then picture what you will do or where you will go when you are dreaming.

4 **Wake up (in your dream).**
You've done everything right, and it turns out that you are, in fact, dreaming and aware of it! Now do what you planned on doing when you went to sleep. Will you swim with dolphins? Will you make the world's biggest pizza? You decide!

Cool Things to Do When You Control Your Dreams

Since you're in dreamland, you can do what you want and the laws of nature (and physics, for that matter) don't apply.

- **Fly.** Whether you "swim" in the air or fly like a superhero, there are few things cooler than looking down on the world your mind has created as the wind blows through your hair.

- **Eat and eat (and eat).** You can make things taste the way you want them to in your dreams. Bite into any object and tell yourself it will taste like chocolate. Guess what? It will.

- **Be amazed.** Simply take in all the cool and crazy things your mind has created.

How to Investigate a Crop Circle

You take the dog out, wait for it to do its business, and let it sniff around that crop circle. *Crop circle?* Crop circles are giant designs in fields of grain made by crushing the stems so they lie flat. Some people think they're made by artsy aliens in flying saucers, but skeptics say they're just fancy hoaxes. So, how do you determine what went down in that field? Channel your inner Sherlock and try these tips.

1. Ask about nighttime noise.

"Circle makers" work at night. So, if a crop circle crops up in your neighborhood wheat or barley field, ask people who live nearby if they heard anything out of the ordinary the night before. Creating a crop circle sometimes involves machinery, like farm vehicles, so someone may have heard something.

2. Get the dirt on the dirt.

To make crop circles, people sometimes use wooden planks to crush the grain stalks. So, examine the dirt in and around the crop circle. Do you see any impressions that look like they were made by a plank being pressed into the dirt? Or, do you see any footprints leading to and from the crop circle?

BE AWARE • So if it wasn't some folks tooling around in a field, who (or what) created the crop circle? Theories include whirlwind vortexes (a type of tornado), ball lightning (mysterious glowing spheres), or military experiments.

Crop Circle Hall of Fame

Though the majority of crop circles have been discovered in southern England, they have also been found in other parts of the world. The four shown below (from a bird's-eye view) vary in size from 198 feet (60 meters) to 916 feet (280 meters) in diameter.

Payerne, Switzerland, July 2007

Tennessee, United States, May 2008

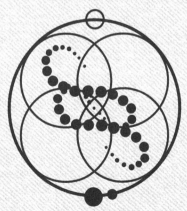

Boryoung City, South Korea, June 2008

Stonehenge, England, July 1996

③ Inspect the center.

To create a perfect circle, crop-circle makers sometimes place a stake in the ground and tie a rope to it. Then they hold the other end of the rope, stretch it tight, and walk in a circle, stomping the grain as they go. To prove that a circle was made this way, look for a little hole in the ground in the exact center of a crop circle. Or, look for a mess of footprints in the center (as someone could have held the rope there). If a neighbor still insists that an alien or UFO did it, just say that your evidence is truly *grounded* in fact. Your work here is done.

Real or Ridiculous?

a. About 10,000 crop circles have been reported worldwide since the 1970s.

b. Some crop circles are made by prairie dog communities.

c. Most formations appear in wheat and corn, but they have also occurred in barley, oats, and grass.

Answer: b. is ridiculous.

CHAPTER 4

Time Travel

How to Pack for Time Travel

So, you somehow figured out the hard part, which is how to travel through time. And your time machine is fueled up and ready to go. It's almost time to take off on your first blast-to-the-past. What do you pack for a trip through centuries? Extra underwear? For sure. What else? Check out the list below.

Time-Travel Kit Essentials

- **Gold.** Today's cash is probably useless where you're headed. Gold, on the other hand, has been valuable across the ages. If you don't have any gold, take along other trade-worthy items, like exotic spices, silks, furs, candy, your brother's toys…

- **Water purifier.** Water hasn't always flowed directly out of faucets, and even when it did, it wasn't always clean. Bad water can mean stomach problems (good thing you've packed that extra underwear).

- **Snacks.** Ancient Romans liked to dine on peacock tongues. In ancient Egypt, the bread was so hard and gritty, it wore down people's teeth. If you won't want to partake in these delights, pack some snacks.

- **Camera.** Want to snap a pic of a not-yet-leaning Tower of Pisa? Shoot a video of Abe Lincoln giving the Gettysburg Address? You'll need a good camera disguise, especially if you want to keep the camera out long enough for video-making.

Camera Disguises for Time Travelers

Wild West diguise

Colonial America disguise

French Revolution disguise

- **First-aid kit.** If you get sick on a trip to the past, you may want to avoid going to the local doctor. In medieval times, medical care was given by barbers, whose remedies included using leeches to "suck out" the sickness. Head back to the future and call your doctor in the morning.

- **Clothes that won't raise eyebrows.** Read up on the fashions of your destination and go for a look that says "I-assure-you-there's-nothing-weird-about-me-at-all."

- **Foreign language dictionary.** You'll want to communicate pressing matters using more than charades or pictures. Just think of all the embarrassing things you might have to act out (like when you really have to go and don't know where to go).

- **History books.** Don't be out of the loop when your new friends talk about "current events." And they'll be oh-so impressed when you predict "the future." Just be sure to travel to a time where you scored at least a "B" on the test about it.

The Weirdest "What If" of Time Travel

What if you traveled to the past and made some change that—gasp!—made it impossible for you to be born?

Imagine it this way: What if you visited the time of your grandfather's youth, and (accidentally, of course!) caused your grandfather to die before he could grow up and start a family? What would happen? Would you disappear right then and there? But wait—how did you exist to get there in the first place?

This famous time-travel puzzler is called "The Grandfather Paradox" ("paradox" means it doesn't make logical sense). Some say this shows that time travel to the past is impossible, because this mind-knotting situation just can't be explained away.

Or can it? Some use a theory called the "Many Worlds Interpretation" to explain it. This theory says that if you traveled to the past and messed up your family tree, you'd create a new, parallel universe in which you would never be born. Poof! A new universe! According to the Many Worlds theory, there could be a different universe for every possible outcome of every possible event. That's a whole lot of universes!

How to Survive a Trip to the Past

When traveling back in time, the key is to blend in. That means: Hide your time machine, act like the locals, know the rules, and play by them. So, if you're chillin' in thirteenth-century Japan and you come across a samurai, you'll know to bow in respect because you studied up on *Bushido*, the samurai's code of honor. Here's a quick time-travel guide for some of history's hot spots.

HOW TO SURVIVE IN PREHISTORIC TIMES

Go back in time 230 to 65 million years, and you're guaranteed to run into a dinosaur or two (or three). Here's how to get a glimpse of these giant prehistoric beasts without ending up a part of the fossil record.

- **Brachiosaurus.** One of the largest animals to walk the earth—it was heavier than 60 elephants. This dino was a plant eater, so don't worry about it chowing down on you. Just don't climb a ginkgo tree to get a look at this guy—it loved to eat branches, so you could get knocked right out.

- **Maiasaura.** Its name means "good mother reptile," but don't expect a lullaby from this duck-billed dino! With nests of around 20 eggs to protect, this big mama is vigilant with a capital V. Since *Maiasaura* is an herbivore, it won't seek you out for dinner. But go near one of its nests, and you'll shoot to the top of its "must destroy" list.

- **Sarcosuchus.** This guy will spy you—and then attack you—from its swampy hideout, so keep an eye out for scaly moving "rocks" and beady eyes.

A relative of the crocodile, this "Supercroc" is the size of a city bus, and five times as heavy any crocodilian creature today.

- **Tyrannosaurus rex.** Use its massive size against it! *T. rex* probably couldn't pounce or change directions quickly, so run in a zigzag pattern to escape its knife-sharp teeth.

What to Eat in Dino Times

If you get hungry, watch what you eat. Many prehistoric plants were probably poisonous. If you do need a quick bite, these are your best bets:

- **Ferns.** The fiddleheads (the fern's leaves before they open) are likely as safe to eat as they are today, but munch them only in moderation. Eating too many can be toxic.

- **Ginkgos.** The nutlike centers are edible—the vomit-smelling flesh surrounding them, not-so-much…

- **Water lilies.** If the ones back then were anything like the ones around today, the roots are safe to eat.

- **Seaweed.** If you land near a coast, seaweed may be plentiful. Most of these plants can be eaten.

- **Honey.** Bees buzzed during the Cretaceous Period (144 to 65 million years ago), so you can always add a dab of honey to your seaweed and ginkgo-nut sandwich.

BE AWARE • Taking a sip of water from a Jurassic stream could make you jura-*sick*! Microscopic parasites lurked in prehistoric water, so be sure to boil water before you drink it. Otherwise, you're risking a dino-sized stomachache!

HOW TO SURVIVE IN ANCIENT ROME

As the saying goes, "When in Rome, do as the Romans do." That's almost all you need to know...

1 Bring your own TP.

Public toilets in ancient Rome often had running water and marble seats, but when it came to toilet paper, well, there wasn't any. Instead, each ancient latrine came

What to wear when in Rome

DON'T
Toga: Worn for formal occasions by Roman citizens only. Foreigners were not allowed to wear them.

ROME MAP

DO
Tunic: The everyday outfit. Safe bet.

with a sponge attached to a stick for all to share. The sponges were rinsed between uses, but still…even the most ready-for-anything time traveler may prefer not to doo as the Romans did.

② Join the crowd.

Your new Roman friends may invite you to a gladiator match in a giant arena called the Colosseum. If that happens, you may find that they—and 50,000 other people—start shouting like crazy folk when one of the gladiators falls to the ground and asks for mercy. If you want to join in (and you want to be nice), yell, "Mitte!" (Mee-tay), which means "Let him go!"

Helpful Latin Phrases

Caveo, ego sum iens vomito! *Cahv-ay-oh, ay-goh soom ee-ayns voom-ee-toh!*	Look out, I'm going to barf!
Tanquam! *Tahn-kwahm!*	As if!
Quis feteo? *Kwees fay-tay-oh?*	What stinks?

HOW TO SURVIVE IN ANCIENT EGYPT

Welcome to the land of pharaohs and pyramids, time traveler! Here are some tips to make your trip as cool as the desert is hot.

① Shave your head.

Having no hair will help keep you cool, but in ancient Egypt, hairstyles also told a lot about a person, including age. Young children had shaved heads except for a long lock of hair on the left side of their heads to signify youth. Adult men and women disguised their shaved heads with wigs. One other advantage to having no hair…no lice!

② Try ancient sunblock.

Men, women, boys, and girls wore face makeup because they liked the look, and it helped protect their skin from the sun. Thick black eyeliner helped protect from the sun's glare, too. So, it wasn't *all* about looking good.

> **BE AWARE** • Most ancient Egyptian kids didn't wear clothes until their teens. The weather was so hot, they didn't need or want them.

Do some pyramid-watching.

The Great Pyramid of Giza has puzzled archaeologists for centuries. How did the ancient Egyptians manage to stack up about 2.3 million giant limestone blocks, each one weighing several tons, when they didn't have any heavy-lifting equipment? Were there ramps? Levers? Or just a whole lot of backaches and blisters? Get yourself a pyramid-side seat and find out!

Solve the mystery of King Tut.

No one knows what killed the young king, who became pharaoh at age 9 and died at 19. Was it murder? A wounded leg that became infected? Ask around, and see if you can get the scoop.

HOW TO SURVIVE IN MEDIEVAL TIMES

If knights and castles are your thing, Europe's Middle Ages (from 1066 to around 1500) might be worth a trip. Just keep in mind—life back then was as tough as the mutton that middle-agers dined on, and few people even reached middle age. Here's how to make the most of your time in medieval times.

1 Avoid the plague like the plague.

There's a nasty flu going around known as the bubonic plague, or the "Black Death." With a name like that, you're dealing with more than a runny nose. In fact, the plague wiped out nearly half of Europe's population. So, wash your hands a lot, stay away from anyone with a cough, and definitely don't hang out with any rats (they carry the disease).

2 Eat at your own risk.

Peasants often ate "black pudding," a dish made with animal blood and fat, milk, onions, and oatmeal. Mmmm, nothing like bloody, fatty, milky oatmeal! Nobles, on the other hand, dined on roasts, fish, and pigeon pie. So, how do you get to dine with the nobles?

Dress the part.

Fake it till you make it with expensive clothing fit for nobility. Hit up a costume store for velvet, furs, and extravagant silk robes. The more color, the more noble.

Joust not.

Anyone can enter a joust, but think twice before donning your armor and hopping on that horse. Many knights were killed in jousting matches, not only by lances but also by their out-of-control steeds.

How to Make the Most of a Trip to the Future

You may know the saying, *Those that fail to learn from history are doomed to repeat it.* Well, the same can be said about the future. If you time travel to the future and discover that things aren't going well—from famine to fashion—you can travel back to the present and save the planet. And you might as well make your life a little sweeter, too.

1 Cash in.

Everyday info in the future translates to big-time cash in the present. Check out which companies are doing well in the stock market. Jot down some winning lottery numbers. When you go back to the present, it won't take much time to build massive wealth (which of course you will donate to charities and worthy causes).

2 Learn your history...er...future lessons.

- **Endangered species.** Rap with future zoologists, entomologists, ecologists, and marine biologists about what's happening in the animal, insect, and plant kingdoms. When you return to the present day, you can help make sure all of the soon-to-be-endangered critters are taken care of.

- **Hot enough for you?** Scientists warn that if we don't do something about climate change, Earth's average temperature will rise a number of degrees by the end of this century. This increase will cause the polar ice caps to continue to melt and sea levels to rise. When you're in the future, find out exactly what has happened and what future scientists think should have been done. Grab as many stats as you can and bring all this information back to the present. Then see if you can help make a positive change.

- **Eureka.** Are there any inventions that you can bring back to help present-day society? Saltwater purifiers to make ocean water drinkable? Flying cars? Maybe there's a new anti-zit cream that you can market at school!

- **Fashion forward.** Bring back some futuristic clothes and be a trendsetter! Make sure to wear your future fashions with confidence, and when asked what era you're channeling, just say the '80s (the 2080s, that is!).

③ Talk to your old self.

As smart as you might be, chances are your older self is a bit wiser about life (especially *your* life). Once you get past the shock of seeing yourself old and wrinkly, ask yourself some questions: Is there anything I should do differently in my life? What is the most important lesson you've (I've) learned? When exactly do I lose all sense of fashion?

Futuristic Fads

Swan-do

Intergalactic League baseball jersey

Cellular jewelry

Blue jeans (always in style)

Nitrogen-propelled sneakers

Real or Ridiculous?
Experts on the Future

What can we expect in the future? People who dedicate their lives to predicting what will happen in the years to come are called "futurists." Can you tell which predictions from the World Future Society (yep, this group exists) are real and which are ridiculous?

a. Koala bears will become domesticated like dogs.

b. Hyper-speed planes will transport passengers at ten times the speed of sound.

c. Ocean currents will generate a lot of our energy.

d. Chemicals found in snails will be among the best new medicines.

e. Cars will run on hydrogen.

f. You will be president.

Answers: a. is ridiculous. Only time will tell with f.

CHAPTER 5

Magic and Myth

How to Run with a Unicorn

There are few mythical creatures as beautiful and mysterious as the unicorn. Though they're difficult to come by—maybe they're embarrassed by the protrusion from their heads?—unicorns have long fascinated humankind, adorning the covers of countless spiral notebooks. A unicorn encounter may be rare, but it's not unlikely, if you follow these tips.

1 Girl power.

According to the usual rules of unicorn lore, the only way to find one is for a fair maiden (sorry, guys) to wait alone where these elusive creatures are suspected to roam, like magical forests or on enchanted riverbanks. When a unicorn sees a maiden of pure heart, it will run up to her and lay its head in her lap. If you're truly pure of heart (Have you been doing your chores? Are you changing the toilet paper roll when you use the last square of TP? Have you stopped drinking milk directly out of the carton?), then you will soon find yourself gently petting a unicorn's silky mane.

2 Born to be wild.

Just because a unicorn nuzzles up against you doesn't mean it's time to break out the leash or the litter box. Unicorns prize their freedom above all else, so don't place it in a stable or fence it in. Instead, let it run freely, preferably in a meadow. Unicorns are loyal and should not run away.

3 Protect and serve.

You aren't the only one with unicorn wishes. About 2,000 years ago, the Greek physician Ctesias claimed that a unicorn horn, if ground up, can prevent sickness. So be on the lookout for unicorn hunters looking to add a little horn dust to their tea.

4 Maintain the mane.

Like horses, unicorns like their manes and coats brushed in order to keep their pearly-white coats ultraclean. Unicorns also like it when you braid their manes and tails. If you're feeling extra adventurous, try to soup up your unicorn with some horse bling, like gold horse-shoes, or knit a cozy to keep your uni's horn warm (and to protect you from being poked).

The Real Deal

Is there a unicorn in Italy? In 2008 in a Florence nature reserve, a young deer received a lot of attention because of its unusual antler. Instead of having a pair of antlers, this deer had one horn sticking straight up from the center of its head. Scientists think that the horn was a rare genetic glitch and that animals like this one might explain reports of unicorn sightings throughout history.

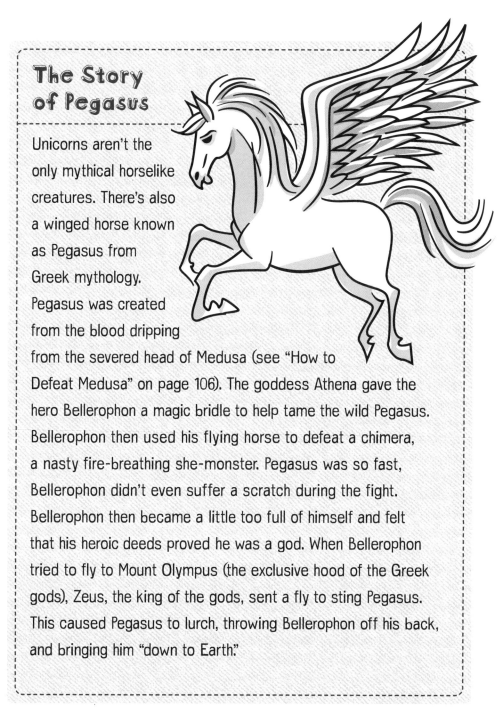

The Story of Pegasus

Unicorns aren't the only mythical horselike creatures. There's also a winged horse known as Pegasus from Greek mythology. Pegasus was created from the blood dripping from the severed head of Medusa (see "How to Defeat Medusa" on page 106). The goddess Athena gave the hero Bellerophon a magic bridle to help tame the wild Pegasus. Bellerophon then used his flying horse to defeat a chimera, a nasty fire-breathing she-monster. Pegasus was so fast, Bellerophon didn't even suffer a scratch during the fight. Bellerophon then became a little too full of himself and felt that his heroic deeds proved he was a god. When Bellerophon tried to fly to Mount Olympus (the exclusive hood of the Greek gods), Zeus, the king of the gods, sent a fly to sting Pegasus. This caused Pegasus to lurch, throwing Bellerophon off his back, and bringing him "down to Earth."

How to Tame and Train a Dragon

Whether they're fire-breathing, ice-spewing, bat-winged, barb-tailed, or yellow-eyed, dragons all have one thing in common: They're equipped to do some serious damage! Here's how to tip their scales in your favor, hop on the dragon wagon, and have the ride of your life!

1 Get the dragon deets.

If you're desperately seeking a dragon's digs, seek out sites high in the mountains, large bodies of freshwater, or caves deep in mossy forests. Still no scales in sight? Your neighborhood wizard may have an idea of where a dragon might be found.

2 Choose your type.

Consult the "Dragon Field Guide" to make sure you're not eyeing an evil dragon. (You won't want to wrangle a wyvern or hang with a Hydra!) The good news is that some dragons are noble and intelligent creatures.

Dragon Field Guide

- **Classic.** These fire breathers can be vicious hoarders of treasure, like Fafnir from Norse mythology and Smaug from the *The Hobbit*, or they can be friendly companions, like Puff.

- **Multiheaded.** Whether it's nine-headed Hydra from Greek mythology or eight-headed Yamata no Orochi from Japanese legend, these dragons are vicious with a capital V!

- **Wyvern.** Often depicted on coats of arms, wyverns are winged dragons that breathe poison instead of flames.

- **Chinese.** Kindhearted with five claws on each foot, Chinese dragons have 117 scales: 81 are infused with good (the yang) and 36 with evil (the yin).

- **Naga.** Indian serpents with the bodies of King Cobras and the heads of humans reward people if they're good and punish them if they're bad—like a snaky Santa Claus.

Dress for success.

Now is not the time to sport your father's flammable polyester suit from the seventies. Suit up in heavy head-to-toe chain-mail armor that will protect you from fiery breath, sharp claws, and gnashing teeth. Chain mail may slow you down, but it's better to be slow than slow-roasted.

4. Plan your approach.

You'll want to stake out your dragon from a safe area. Bring binoculars and get to know its habits. Don't be surprised if you spot it surrounded by mounds of gold and shiny gemstones because all smart adventurers know to…

5. Come bearing gifts.

Gold, silver, rubies, and diamonds are a dragon's best friends, so you may need to "borrow" some of your mom's jewelry. Approach the dragon *very* slowly, always keeping some distance between you. Stay behind your shield as the dragon surveys your gift. As the dragon checks out your irresistible offering, it should be less interested in considering *you* a tasty prize.

6. Scale the scales.

Now that you've made friends, it's time to fly! When the dragon crouches down, don't take a minute to consider your options—dragons don't like to ask twice. Accept the invitation promptly by hopping onto its back, eventually settling on its shoulders. Hold its neck tightly because you're about to do some serious soaring!

How to Find and Befriend a Fairy

A fairy, faery, or fairie is a magical, mischievous, delicate little creature who can't seem to pick a spelling and stick with it. Having the appearance of a miniature person (wings are optional), a fairy can be a trusted friend in times of need, but it can also be a pest and make mischief if you break some fairy rules. Here's how to fare well with a fairy…faery…or fairie.

1. Believe. Believe. Believe.

The key to securing fairy friendship is believing that fairies exits. In *Peter Pan*, J.M. Barrie wrote, "Every time a child says 'I don't believe in fairies' there is a fairy somewhere that falls down dead." You definitely don't want that to happen, so follow Pete's advice: Clap your hands and say, "I believe in fairies!" to keep them alive and to increase your odds of finding one.

2. Plant a seed.

To attract your garden-variety fairies, fill your garden with their favorite flowers and plants, like foxgloves, ferns, and primroses. Tulips make cozy beds for fairy babies, and if you're up at the crack of dawn, you might catch a glimpse of these tiny tots. You can also build a fairy house (similar to a bird house) with twigs and rocks. Fairies like sparkle, so add some crystals and beads.

Signs a Fairy Might Be Nearby

- A whisper in the leaves
- The tinkling of bells
- The appearance of a pretty feather
- A sudden pleasant smell

3 Go mushroom hunting.

Some legends say that a ring of mushrooms is formed by fairies dancing in a circle and is a portal to a fairy world. And if you skip around a mushroom ring nine times on the night of a new moon, you may hear sounds from that magical world. In any case, where there are mushrooms, there's a good chance there are fairies (the mushrooms on your pizza don't count).

> **BE AWARE** • If you visit the fairy world, don't eat or drink anything. If you do, the rules of fairy lore say you have to stay in fairy land forever!

4 Churn some butter.

According to English folklore, good fairies love butter, and you can summon one by making butter while chanting, "Come, butter, come. Come, butter, come. Peter stands at the gate, waiting for a buttered cake. Come, butter, come!" If that doesn't work...

5 Bring out the sweets.

Fairies love sweet things, especially honey. Pour some honey on a plate and leave it on your front steps or windowsill. You could also try leaving fruit like currants (a fairy favorite). Don't be insulted if a fairy only takes a quick nibble and then flies off. Keep providing the goodies, and the fairies should grow to trust you.

6 What's the catch?

Never catch or trap a fairy, or the fairy and its friends will wreak havoc on your life in the form of pranks and mischief.

Fairy Trouble

Not all stories about fairies are pleasant ones. During the nineteenth century, fairies were blamed for all kinds of mischief, such as tangling people's hair and stealing small objects. To ward off these "evil fairies," believers wore iron charms, turned their clothes inside out, and left out stale bread. Of course, blaming "evil fairies" comes in handy when you've cut the cheese!

How to Defeat Medusa

Imagine a creature so ghastly, so utterly repulsive, that the mere sight of her will turn you to stone. With serpentine hair that slithers and hisses, Medusa puts the "Ugh!" in ugly. Many a hero tried to take down the nasty hag, only to find himself turned into a permanent fixture in her lair. Finally, someone figured out how to tackle this stone-cold killer. Here's the secret, in case you're unlucky enough to run into Medusa II.

1 **Don't look now.**

If you think *you're* having a bad hair day, take a look at Medusa's locks for some perspective. Wait! Don't! If you look directly at this snake-haired Gorgon, or even sneak a peek, you'll turn to stone faster than you can say "Gross." Medusa's lair is a bona fide art museum full of sculptures of people who were foolish enough to lay their eyes on her. So how exactly *are* you supposed to defeat Medusa if you can't even look at her?

2 **Use a shield.**

In Greek mythology, the hero Perseus was charged with the task of beheading Medusa. His secret weapon? A very shiny bronze shield that was given to him

Beauty Before Beast

Medusa wasn't always an eyesore! She was once a beautiful woman who prized her beautiful ringlets of hair above all else. But when the dashing damsel upset the goddess Athena, Athena turned her locks into serpents, transforming the once beautiful Medusa into a hideous monster.

by the Goddess of Wisdom, Athena. Using his reflective shield, Perseus was able to see his target without looking directly at her. Unless Athena is a friend of the family, you'll probably want to visit your local blacksmith and ask for a specially made, highly polished bronze shield (and a nice sharp sword while you're at it). Or, just snatch a mirror off your living room wall.

③ Shield, shield, on the wall.

As you make your way into Medusa's lair, listen closely. You should soon hear the hissing of Medusa's serpentine hairdo. Once you're in striking distance, lean your reflective shield against the wall. And wait.

④ Sneak, step, and strike.

You want to take Medusa by surprise, so use the statues of her victims to hide behind (they won't mind!). Then be still. When Medusa's face appears in your shield, brace yourself (she is not a pretty sight!). Once she gets in range, step out from behind your statue, close your eyes tightly, and swing for the neck.

Other Mythological Creatures on Your To-Slay List

- **Minotaur.** The Athenian king Theseus took down this half-bull–half-man beast with a magic sword, but killing Minotaur is only half the battle. You also need to escape the labyrinth built by the master-builder Daedalus.

- **Cyclops.** This giant has one eye smack-dab in the middle of its forehead. Take a cue from the hero Odysseus, who managed to escape the cyclops Polyphemus by striking its eye with a stake.

- **Chimera.** With the body of a goat, the head of a lion, and the tail of a serpent, this she-monster breathes fire. In order to take her down, you need to strike from a distance, using a bow and arrow, like the hero Bellerophon (see "The Story of Pegasus" on page 97).

How to Be a Sorcerer's Apprentice

Sorcery isn't all fun and magic wands. Most spells are cast using ancient languages, and speaking them correctly demands hours of study and learning from a master. Here's how to be a star student.

1 **Don't be afraid to get your hands dirty.**
Alchemy, or the mixing of potions, is an important part of becoming a sorcerer. Potions are often made up of unappealing ingredients, like wriggling spider legs, lizard eyes, and snake tongues. If you're squeamish, start slow. Work up from one spider leg to three. Before you know it, nothing will faze you.

2 **Spell-check before you spell-wreck.**
Make sure you practice magic only under your teacher's supervision. Spells can have significant consequences if cast incorrectly. You may *think* you're reciting a spell to conjure up a hamburger, only to mispronounce a word and summon a hobgoblin.

From the Vault: Merlin the Magnificent

Merlin, the wizard from the legend of King Arthur, was a sorcerer and advisor to King Arthur and his Round Table, a group of the bravest knights in the kingdom. Later, Merlin fell for an enchantress who tricked him into teaching her all of his magic. She then imprisoned him in a tree—not exactly the nicest way to thank your teacher.

How to Get What You Want from a Genie

Just like Aladdin in *One Thousand and One Nights*, you're polishing a tarnished antique oil lamp, when all of a sudden you are looking up into the twinkling eyes of a bejeweled figure who exclaims, "Your wish is my command!" Of course, you like the sound of those five words. Just be careful what you wish for…

1 Think before wishing.

A genie often grants wishes in ways that cause the wisher to wish he'd never wished the wish in the first place (try saying *that* three times in a row!). So, make sure the wording of your wish is crystal clear with lots of details and no room for a second (or third) interpretation.

2 Make your last wish count.

Often the best last wish is to undo the first two wishes or to wish the genie back into the lamp, so he can't cause any more trouble. Oh, and the whole "I wish for more wishes" bit won't fly with genies. That's on their "Do not grant" list, so don't even try!

What You Might Wish for... and What You Might Get!

- **To be able to fly.** The genie makes you afraid of heights.

- **To be a rock star.** The genie makes you a geologist who studies rocks all day.

- **To be rich.** The genie turns you into delectable milk chocolate.

How to Swim with a Mermaid

You're out deep-sea fishing, and nothing's biting. You decide to chill out, lean back, and take in the wide expanse of the deep blue sea. Suddenly, you see a large tail fin break the water in the distance. As you survey the splash, you see long blond hair on the water's surface. Are your eyes playing tricks on you, or is it the ever-elusive mermaid—your biggest catch of the day?

Far out, dude!

You're not gonna find a mermaid batting a beach ball around at the local beach. According to folklore, merfolk live deep beneath the sea. They prefer to swim among rocky coves and caverns far from any popular beaches and sea routes—though they may swim upriver to freshwater lakes. Ask experienced seafarers where mermaids are rumored to be. Next thing you know, you'll be yelling, "Mermaid, ho!"

Listen up.

Once you're headed toward Mermaidville, listen up. Mermaids are known for their beautiful singing. Head toward the sound, but be careful! The song may be coming from a Siren, a mischievous seafaring creature that's half-bird–half-human. Sirens' songs enchant sailors and place them under a spell, causing sailors to walk off ship decks or to crash their ships into rocks.

BE AWARE • Every sailor worth his sea salt knows not to harm a mermaid. Legend says that if you do, a terrible storm will rage, endangering your ship and crew.

Rock out.

If you've got some pipes, try coaxing a mermaid to emerge by singing a little ditty of your own. Mermaids prefer the peacefulness of the sea, so don't belt out any heavy metal. Choose a classic sea chantey instead, like "Blow the Man Down" or "Good-bye, Fare Thee Well." Mermaids will only be attracted to a pleasant voice— they're the ultimate talent show judges. (Plus, you don't want to be pelted by seashells. Ouch!)

The Little Mermaid

What a mermaid will do for love! In Hans Christian Andersen's tale, "The Little Mermaid," a beautiful mermaid is willing to trade her cushy life in an underwater paradise for the love of a handsome prince on land. Because she drinks a potion that changes her fin to legs, the mermaid is never allowed back to her watery paradise. This story gives a whole new meaning to "sea legs."

How to Outwit a Leprechaun

Sometimes, little things can be big trouble. Such is the case with the leprechaun, a wily little Irishman full of mischief and mind tricks. If you can manage to outwit him, though, you could find yourself with a big ol' pot o' gold.

1 Here's the catch.
Legend says that leprechauns live in hollows under trees or in furnished caves. Rather than squeezing yourself into an uncomfortably small place, you'll want to lure one *your* way. Prop up a box supported by a stick connected to a long string. Under the box, leave your bait: either something gold (leprechauns like to add to their pot) or an old shoe (leprechauns are cobblers by nature, so they can't resist a shoe in need of repair).

BE AWARE • Leprechauns were originally known for wearing red clothing, not green.

② Have a staring contest.

Watch your trap like a hawk. Leprechauns may be small—they're only 2 feet (60 centimeters) tall—but they're fast. When you see the leprechaun take the bait, pull the string, allowing the box to fall and cover him. Remove the box and lock your gaze on the man o' mischief, or he'll vanish.

③ Strike a deal.

Leprechauns may be tricky, but they're also o'-so predictable: When you catch one, he'll probably want to trade his freedom for information about his pot o' gold. According to leprechaun lore, as long as you look the leprechaun in the eye when you make the deal, he should tell you where the gold is buried.

BE AWARE • A leprechaun may try to bribe you before giving up the information about his pot o' gold. Don't fall for any of his tricks, including the offer of a gold coin. It will turn to dust once you release him.

Trick and No Treat

There are many tales about leprechauns outwitting humans. In one famous story, a leprechaun told the man who caught him that his pot o' gold was buried under a bush. The man then tied a red ribbon to the bush. The leprechaun promised that he would not remove the ribbon or the gold. When the man returned with a shovel to claim his prize, he found that the leprechaun had tied red ribbons to hundreds of bushes.

How Not to Get Crushed by a Giant

So you know how to deal with the little guys and gals—leprechauns and fairies—but what about the big fellas? Just like their name, giants are, well, giant. Some can be friendly, but most would like to crush you, then eat you, and use your little bones as toothpicks. Here's how to avoid being tonight's appetizer.

① Duck and cover.

On open ground, you can't outrun a giant. One of their steps equals ten of yours, and a well-placed one will squash you like an ant. But if you're in a forest or indoors, you can duck in and out of nooks and crannies where a giant can't fit.

② Fee fi toe fum.

Most giants don't wear shoes, leaving their feet vulnerable to an attack. Being vertically challenged, you can't help but stare at a giant's ugly toes. Jab right between them—where the stinky toe jam lives—with a stick, or slam down a stone squarely on one of his toenails. Then run and hide!

A Tall Tale

"Jack and the Beanstalk" shows that brains (and greed) can prevail over brawn. Jack successfully climbed the stalk twice—nabbing gold and a hen that laid golden eggs—but the third time wasn't quite a charm. When the giant caught wind of Jack, Jack took down the stalk and the ogre with an axe...and lived happily ever after.

Appendix

FIELD GUIDE TO MAGICAL WOODLAND CREATURES

When a quest takes you deep into the magical forest, you'll want to know how to deal with the creatures that dwell there. Here are some of the usual suspects.

- **Elves.** A far cry from the vertically challenged toy makers from the North Pole, these pointy-eared, quick, and wise elves can be of great help to any adventurer. Elves are said to be immortal and have magical abilities, including great healing powers. Elvish singing (not to be confused with Elvis!) can raise the spirits of those who are wounded or those who are feeling down in the dumps. Elves also have hawklike vision and are able to see in the dark, making them great scouts for any adventurer's party.

- **Dwarves**. The short and stocky linebackers of woodland creatures, dwarves often sport beards and heavy armor and are skilled with axes. These master metalsmiths will offer you magical weapons and armor (for the right payment, of course).

- **Trolls.** These big dudes aren't going to win any woodland creature beauty pageants! They have tough skin, long noses, questionable hygiene, and animal-carcass breath. Trolls won't eat humans, but they *are* known to hurl rocks at passersby.

- **Gnomes**. Gnomes are tiny little guys (smaller than a newborn baby) who wear pointed hats that are nearly as tall as they are. They are peaceful creatures who guard the animals of the forest, freeing them from traps and tending to the injured.

FORM FOR DOCUMENTING A UFO SIGHTING

Date: _____ _____ , _____ Time: _____ a.m./p.m.
          (Month)   (Day)   (Year)

Location: _____ , _____ , _____
               (Street name)   (City)   (Country)

UFO'S CHARACTERISTICS: Shape: _____

Color: _____ Describe movement: _____

Other: _____

Sketch of UFO:

Alien sighting with ship?
Sketch of alien:

UNUSUAL PHENOMENA AT TIME OF SIGHTING:

❏ Street lights flickering on and off

❏ Your hair sticking up more than usual

❏ Other _____

ANIMALS ACTING STRANGELY:

❏ Parrots squawking "Take me to your leader"

❏ Cats chasing dogs

❏ Other _____

FORM FOR DOCUMENTING A BIZARRE-CREATURE SIGHTING

Date: _____ _____ , _____ Time: _____ a.m./p.m.
      (Month)   (Day)   (Year)

Location: _____ , _____ , _____
      (Street name)   (City)   (Country)

Appearance and unusual features: _____

Describe creature's movements: _____

What was creature doing at time of sighting?: _____

_____

Smell:

❏ New car smell   ❏ Blend of old sneakers and morning breath

❏ Finely aged dog poop   ❏ Other _____

Describe creature's noises: _____

Sketch of creature:

Sketch of creature's tracks:

Sketch of creature's poo:

About the Experts

These experts reviewed select tips in this handbook and offered smart advice. Consider them the wizards of weird!

Rachel Connolly is the director of the Gheens Science Hall and Rauch Planetarium at the University of Louisville. She was previously the Education Manager at the American Museum of Natural History's Hayden Planetarium in New York City, and, before that, a high school physics teacher in the Bronx. She is currently completing her Ph.D. at Columbia University's Teachers College where she has held a NASA Graduate Fellowship.

Carl Mehling is a paleontology collections manager in a natural history museum and he has been fascinated by fossils since childhood. Carl has collected fossils around the world, and sees no end to the surprises offered by the fossil record. Carl spends a good amount of time traveling to study the organisms of Earth's past.

About the Authors

David Borgenicht is the coauthor and creator of all the books in the Worst-Case Scenario series. He has never encountered vampires, zombies, or ghosts but claims to have seen Bigfoot in the mountains outside of Salt Lake City, Utah, where he grew up. Then again, it might just have been a really hairy fellow camper.

Justin Heimberg has, from time to time, been considered weird. Maybe it's because he creates "art" by wrapping pieces of used gum around a coat hanger. Then again, maybe it's just because he is weird, a label he welcomes with great cheerfulness.

About the Illustrator
Chuck Gonzales is very pleased to be involved with another Worst-Case Scenario Junior edition. Especially one with zombies, vampires, and aliens. Although he's never had to fight any off, knowledge is power!